TABLE OF CONTENTS

Chapter 1: History of Butte

Chapter 2: Appetizers/Others

Chapter 3: Main Dishes

Chapter 4: Sides

Chapter 5: Breads

Chapter 6: Desserts

Chapter 7: Hints

CHAPTER 1
HISTORY

This is a collection of hundreds of recipes tested over many years from friends and family in Butte, Montana, which are just as vividly delightful and colorful as the history of Butte. The history is flavored by an enormous variety of ethnicities who came to work in the highly profitable copper mines at the turn of the 20th century.

These legacies are evidenced in the magnificent homes of the rich and huge brick uptown buildings, the widow makers dotting the existence of the underground mines where men plunged deep into the darkness of the earth and where some never returned from, and later the world's largest open toxic mining pit, but just as most importantly in the food.

Growing up in Butte, you learned well that food brought people together and made friends for life perhaps necessitated by the harshness of living conditions and a passionate need of the Butte people to live life to the fullest. Nobody was better at making friends for life with food than my family, especially my grandmother Lil, mother Myrna, and Aunt Donna who were known locally as some of the best cooks but even more importantly as some of the best company fully celebrating holidays and enjoying late-night poker games though the stakes were never high.

The history of Montana could not be told without telling about the vividly colorful and sometimes sordid history of Butte and the treasures that still remain there within the buildings, the people, and their food. This book unfolds those treasures of Butte through the sharing of the most sure way to make to make lifelong friends and good neighbors– food with unequalled notoriety.

(miningartifacts.org)

Though a reputation as tough and stark as the arsenic that once consumed the nylons on women's legs, leaving them bare as well as the landscape dotted with widow makers, Butte remains a hidden historical treasure with a highly colorful past wherein its secrets are hidden in the underground mines and under their old monstrous buildings but even more so in the tales of and by its colorful people.

Butte truly earned its reputation as a "town too tough to die" despite many great odds against it. This tough reputation was clearly described by David in the movie, 'Sabrina", when he descries that if he misbehaves he will be exiled to Butte.

> "See, father will want to send me to Larrabee Copper in Butte, Montana, and we don't want to go to Butte Montana, do we?"

Some of Butte's tough reputation is well earned because the town has bred through generations tough people who had to be to survive bitter cold winters with temperatures dipping to 40 below and a living etched out of the mines far underground and the toxic air above polluted with the sulfurous smoke from the Anaconda smelter, and not least of all, the scandalous and seedy lifestyles and politics which earned Butte the title of "the Sodom of the West" by Walter Winchell (Les Rickey,). Later, Butte earned the title of "a mile high and a mile deep" due to its high altitude and the vast open mining pit. (Picture: montanakids.com)

THE PEOPLE

They came to Butte from everywhere, beginning with the Cornish followed by the Irish, Italians, Serbians, Finns, Germans, and many others ethnicities. They maintained their ethnic and cultural roots through living together in their own sections known as Finntown, McQueen, Meaderville, Walkerville, Centerville, Dublin Gulch, Chinatown, Corktown, and Parrot Flat. Parts of these cultures remain alive today in Butte in the foods, buildings, customs and celebrations with St. Patty's Day being one of the biggest holidays still with bars, such as the infamous M&M, packed with people.

These immigrants and their ancestors embodied the toughness of Butte. Boys were known as Tiny and Tank which was not necessarily due to size but to their strength and toughness; perhaps it is this that instilled fear about Butte and a reputation as a tough town, but then they always won whether it was a football game or a fight.

Characteristic of the girth and strength of the boys from Butte was Milo Casagrande who owned a premier wrecker service. Those who worked for him told stories of how when he was over 50 years old he would outwork any young guy cleaning up the scenes of overturned wrecks.

The people were made even tougher by the seedy politics and the parasitic nature of those who took from the "richest hill on earth", sending its wealth back east and into Europe. In the early 1900's, Butte was producing "more mineral wealth than any other mining district in the world up to the middle of the 20th century …[which] spawned the most influential labor market anywhere [resulting in strong labor unions which earned Butte the nickname "the Gibraltar of Unionism."], the most ethnically diverse population in the country, the largest red light district in the American West, nine railroads, the largest network of underground workings per square mile in the world (over 10,000 miles of tunneling), more wealth per citizen than any other comparable place up to that time" and a population of over 100,000 in the early 1900's. (westernmininghistory.com)

The seedy politics was fueled by the War of the Copper Kings (Daly and Clark (who was known as the second richest man in America second only to Rockefeller and whose home, the Copper King Mansion, is pictured below). With the mines came the unions which produced

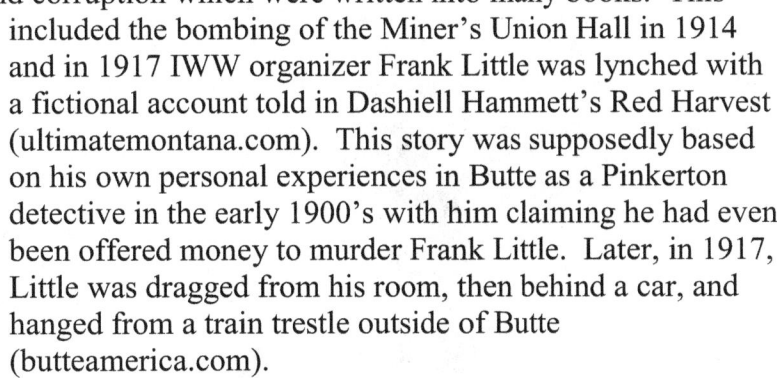

many infamous stories of violence and corruption which were written into many books. This included the bombing of the Miner's Union Hall in 1914 and in 1917 IWW organizer Frank Little was lynched with a fictional account told in Dashiell Hammett's Red Harvest (ultimatemontana.com). This story was supposedly based on his own personal experiences in Butte as a Pinkerton detective in the early 1900's with him claiming he had even been offered money to murder Frank Little. Later, in 1917, Little was dragged from his room, then behind a car, and hanged from a train trestle outside of Butte (butteamerica.com).

Copperkingmansion.com

The parasitic nature of the distant rich and the federal government, and in particular the War of the Copper Kings, fueled the politics of Montanans who have always begrudged the distance between them and those who controlled their lives and stole their riches with a long-lasting underlying fervor to become their own country. "Almost all Montanans resented the far-removed national government" (Toole, 97). In all of this politics, Butte was a primary player from the beginning in the early 1900's when most political power came from Butte, even unto today where many call it Butte America.

I remember growing up in Butte in the 60's and 70's that life was tough with the townspeople never able to get out of debt because just when they got out of debt, as predictable as ever, there would be another strike and once again the people were without work or money. K. Ross Toole, the foremost historian and writer on the history of Montana, (1959) described it well, "For every sudden rise, a sudden fall. Optimism has alternated almost monotonously with despair" (p.9). Butte's perseverance to exist truly earned it a title of a town to tough to die.

Even into the 60's and 70's, Butte's seedy politics and corruption continued. Because of the great inter-generational history and familiarity amongst Butte families in a town that had dwindled down to about 30,000 people, it was very disturbing when several Butte cops (Sullivan, Labreche, Markovich and others) who we had grown up with were robbing and threatening us at gunpoint including my grandfather and brother who worked the Wells Fargo Armored truck which was robbed early one morning in November 1973. Many Butte families experienced similar threats by these cops which included a staggering rate of three burglaries per day in 1975 (Les Rickey). These families included Hannifin's Jewelry store, Buttrey's, Christie's, Skagg's Drugstore, Brinck's, Perino's, Trevillion, the Corner Bar, and Golden Rule Store, the people and places all very familiar to anyone from Butte.

THE BUILDINGS

Nowhere is the triumph of the Butte spirit more evident than today in which the townspeople have brilliantly remodeled and restored through their own sweat and perseverance many of their magnificent and historic buildings earning them the title of the second largest National Historic Landmark District in the country.

RED LIGHT DISTRICT: Prostitution was a booming business in Butte from its origins in uptown Butte on Mercury Street as seen today in the Dumas building which has been reputed to be the "longest-running house of prostitution in the U.S. In the brick alley behind the brothel was the equally famous Venus Alley where women plied their trade in small cubicles called "cribs". The red-light district brought miners and other men from all over the region and was open until 1982 as one of the last such urban districts in the U.S." (Wikipedia.org). Charlie Chaplin recalled in his 1964 book My Autobiography, "Butte boasted of having the prettiest women of any red-light district in the West, and it was true. If one saw a pretty girl smartly dressed, one could rest assured she was from the red-light quarter, doing her shopping." (Buttecvb.com)

For those of us in the 60's and 70's of Butte, this history of prostitution was vividly lived in the personage of the former madam, Dirty Mouth Jean Sorenson, who owned and managed the Stockman's Bar. The last tale told of her in 1978 was when three soldiers stopped in her bar and when she refused to serve them, they became belligerent and confronted her. It was then that she brought out her gun from behind the bar and began shooting, killing one for which she was found guilty. Her comment about the shooting was "I'm slowing down in my old age. There was a time when I'd have gotten all three of them" (Les Rickey). Roadhaus.com

BARS: Bars have always been a standard fixture of the history of Butte including underground bars with endless tales and drinking, particularly on St. Patty's. Nowhere in town was this more celebrated than at the infamous M& M Bar with sordid tales of how rough and dirty it was with people passing out and being swept up off the floors after the bars closed at 2 am, so I was told. Jack Kerouac described well the people in the M&M: " What characters in there: old prospectors, gamblers, whores, miners,

Indians, cowboys, tobacco-chewing businessmen! Groups of sullen Indians drank rotgut in the john. Hundreds of men played cards in an atmosphere of smoke and spitoons. It was the end of my quest for an ideal bar..."

THEATERS: In its early days, Butte had seven absolutely gorgeous theaters with big names performing in them including Charlie Chaplin, Fred Astaire, Bob Hope and many others. I remember as a child going to the Fox Theater and the Montana Theater but these theaters, as all of them, fell into disrepair; however, the Fox Theater was fully restored in the 70's and its original name, Mother Lode Theater, restored. (marcmoss.net)

COLUMBIA GARDENS: Nearest and dearest to the people of Butte was the gift to the people from Copper King Clark in 1899 known as Columbia Gardens – the most elegant of amusement parks with magnificent and glowingly white buildings including a dance pavilion, wooden roller coaster and handcrafted carousel "which was considered the 'crowned jewel' since it was designed by Allen Herschel in 1928" (www.rollercoastersofthepacificnw.com). Kids would pile onto the city buses during the hot summers in the 60s and 70s and be transported to a most magical throwback to the days of elegance and charm that Columbia Gardens was since its origins.

Even as a child we could understand that the old-fashioned charm remained priceless and we savored every moment there including the unique horse swings and umbrella swings whose sole purpose was for all of us kids to swing around as fast as we could in hopes of throwing everyone else off but in fear that we would be the one who flew off and ended up seriously hurt as the swing gained extreme momentum for our playgrounds were not built for safety but for bravery.

In amongst this, the immaculately white grandeur of the buildings shone amongst the beautiful gardens where we first discovered as a child that they shape greenery into animals and flowers abounded everywhere; where we thrilled at the creaks of the old wood of the buildings and walkways as well as of the huge roller coaster; where we pondered for long times as to which handcrafted magnificent horse we would hopefully get on the carousel.

lemonymommy.blogspot.com

FIRES: In the 70's, a great community event became the many convenient fires that consumed the old historic buildings in uptown Butte including the Pennsylvania Building, Penney's Store, and the Medical Arts Building. These fires were so frequent, costly and assuredly arson-related that insurance companies left town and Butte was assigned an unheard level 5 rating for fire risk as well as having the dubious distinction of being the city with the highest number of fires per capita at that time (Les Rickey, "The Bad Boys of Butte", 2004).

SADDLE CLUB: My Aunt Alice was the secretary of the Saddle Club in Butte which hosted the Rodeo every year in addition to various other event and groups. One of those most affectionately valued groups was The Petticoat Patrol of which Aunt Alice was a member and the Sheriff's Posse of which Grandpa Ted was a member.

With my aunt's great involvement in the Saddle Club, all of us kids as teenagers spent much of our time there as well including attending the dances where John Raymond's band of teenage friends played, the mucking out rain-soaked manure from corrals, and the frying and selling of hamburgers during the rodeo, the smell of both which remained in our noses and on your clothes for days. Most memorable were the rodeos where we did many things including when Cousin Duane helped our grandpa with watching the fence during the brahma bull rides so the bulls couldn't get out, except sometimes they came very close and one time a bull did get out and began chasing my cousin and grandpa. Many thanks to the clowns who could sway a bull away from any interest he had focused on.

As you journey throughout this book into the historic buildings, people and recipes of Butte, Montana, the one thing that will be undeniable is that David in the movie "Sabrina" and all of the others who never gave Butte credit were wrong for they didn't know Butte because they had never lived there - for its color in its history, buildings, and people but particularly in its food which are all unforgettable and worth cherishing.

This Book is dedicated to my cousin Devvi Morgan, my sister Rebecca Johnson, and the Three Sisters, Alice, Donna and Myrna Miller, and their mother, Lillian with thanks for the pictures and recipes in this book .

Reprinted, February 20, 2013
Copyright December 2, 2011, by Lynette Olsen, Ph.D. All rights reserved.
The Three Sisters Educational and Administrative Services
www.tseas.wordpress.com
This material may not be duplicated for any profit-driven enterprise.

CHAPTER 2
APPETIZERS/EXTRAS

Soda Punch   Pour 1 2 liter of ginger ale or other light colored soda into punch bowl. Add 1 container of sherbet and frozen juice any flavor. Add ice.

Bridge Mix
Myrna Miller

2 c. butter melted; add 2 tablespoons Worcestershire sauce, 1 tablespoon garlic powder, 1 tablespoon Tabasco, 2 # mixed nuts, 1-12 oz box of wheat chex, 1 small rice check box, 1-10 oz box of cheerios, box of pretzels. Bake 2 hours at 250 degrees, then stir.

Pineapple Party Punch
Donna Ericson

1 can (46 oz.) pineapple juice, chilled
3 cups cranberry juice cocktail, chilled
1 quart ginger ale, chilled
1 cup light rum, if desired
1 lemon, thinly sliced

Combine pineapple juice, cranberry juice cocktail and ginger ale in a large punch bowl. Stir in rum if desired. Float lemon slices on top. Freeze 7 up or ginger ale in a ring mold and put in punch bowl first, then add other juice, etc. Add rum if desired. Float lemon slices

Margaritas

Dev's:
1 sm. can limeade (undiluted) , 3 oz. tequila, 1 1/2 oz.
   Triple Sec. Fill blender with ice and blend till slush. We used this recipe on 7/22/98 when Fred and Kathy came for dinner. We had 36 oz. of liquor and used 4 limeade circles in the ice shaver. It was plenty! And good!

Original:
3 sm. Dixie cups tequila, 1 sm. Dixie cup Triple
   Sec, 1 sm. can limeade (undiluted), 16 ice cubes.

By the Pitcherful: 1 1/2 cups tequila, 1 cup fresh lime juice,
   1/2 cup Triple Sec.

Carol Olsen: 1 shot tequila, 1/2 shot cointreau, 1 shot sweet
   and sour, 1/2 shot lime juice.

Basic Frozen Margaritas: lime wedge, coarse salt, 6 oz. tequila (3/4 cup), 4 oz. frozen limeade concentrate (1/2 cup), 1/3 cup Triple Sec, 20-24 ice cubes (about 3 cups). Moisten rims of glasses with lime; invert into coarse salt. Chill glasses. In blender container combine the tequila, limeade concentrate, and liqueur. Cover; blend smooth. With blender running, add ice cubes, one at a time, blending till slushy. Pour into prepared glasses. Serves 8

Note: For the following variations, prepare glasses as above or use granulated sugar instead of the salt.
   Very Berry Margarita: In blender container combine the tequila, limeade concentrate and liqueur. Add one 1 10oz. pkg. frozen strawberries, broken up. Cover and blend till smooth. Add ice as directed for Basic Frozen Margaritas.
   Gorgeous Grape Margarita: In blender container combine the tequila, one 6 oz. can frozen grape juice concentrate and liqueur; cover and blend till smooth. Omit limeade concentrate. Add ice as directed for the Basic Frozen Margaritas.
   Banana Margarita: In blender container combine the tequila, limeade concentrate, liqueur, and 2 cups cut-up ripe bananas; cover and blend till smooth. Add ice as directed for Basic Frozen Margaritas.
   Apricotta Margarita: In blender container combine the tequila, limeade concentrate, liqueur, and one 16 oz. can apricot halves or peach slices, drained; blend till smooth. Add ice as directed for Basic Frozen Margaritas.

Another Margarita version: 4 servings
1 lime wedge + 4 lime wedges for garnish
Kosher salt
4 oz. Tequila
4 oz. Cointreau
4 oz. fresh lime juice
8-10 ice cubes, crushed

Moisten rims of 4 glasses with lime wedge. Dip glasses in salt. In large pitcher combine tequilla, Cointreau, lime juice and ice. Stir to mix. Let stand several minutes. Pour into glasses and garnish with lime wedge.

Hot Spiced Wine
Donna Ericson

Boil for 5 minutes:
- 1/2 cup water
- 1 cup sugar
- 2 whole cloves
- 2 cinnamon sticks
- 1/2 lemon sliced

Strain and add to 4 cups fruit juice (orange or cranberry) and 1 quart (or more) of cheap burgundy wine. Heat. Can be kept warm in crock pot.

Banana Punch
Donna Ericson

Boil and cool:
3 cups water
2 cups sugar

Add 46 oz. pineapple juice
1 1/2 cups orange juice
1/4 cup lemon juice and 3 bananas which have been blended in
    blender
Pour into 2 - 1/2 gallon containers and freeze.

20 - 30 minutes before serving, remove from freezer and add 3 quarts 7 Up, ginger ale or sparkling water (any will do).
Makes 24 - 36 4 oz. glasses.

Eggnog
Michelle Hunt

Never a better eggnog!
2 c milk
½ c. sugar
½ envelope gelatin

Dissolve gelatin in ¼ c water. Scald milk and sugar stirring constantly. Separate 3 eggs; whip yolks with fork. Add yolks and gelatin to hot milk and sugar Add a little hot milk to yolks so they won't cook in hot milk. Let yolks, milk, sugar and gelatin boil about a minute stirring constantly. Take off stove and let set up in freezer until like a jello. Beat eggs whites til stiff then add ¼ c sugar and eat some more. Beat ½ pint whipping cream. Add egg whites and whipping cream to firm set up mixture. Add rum if desired. Let set up more and add milk.

Chili Cheese Squares
Donna Ericson

Cut into small squares for hors d' oeuvres or large ones for a brunch or luncheon entree

4 T. (1/2 stick) butter
5 eggs
1/4 cup flour
1/2 pint whole or low fat small curd cottage cheese (1 cup)

1/2 t. baking powder
dash salt
1 can (4 oz.) chopped green chilies
2 cups shredded Monterey Jack cheese

Preheat oven to 400 degrees. Melt butter in a 9 inch square pan in oven.
Tip pan to coat bottom with melted butter. In a large bowl beat eggs. Stir in flour, baking powder and salt. Stir in chilies, cottage cheese and Jack cheese. Stir in melted butter until blended. Turn batter into butter coated pan. Bake 15 minutes. Reduce heat to 350 degrees and bake for 30 to 35 minutes longer or until lightly browned. Cool slightly and cut into small squares for appetizers or large squares for entrees. (Squares may be frozen and reheated at 400 degrees before serving. Makes 32 appetizers or 4 entrees.

Variation: Recipe may be doubled and baked in a 13x9 inch baking dish.
One package (10 oz.) frozen chopped
spinach, thawed and drained, may be added
with the chilies.

Hoppin' Johnny
Donna Ericson

1 - 15 1/2 oz. can black-eyed peas, drained
2 cups cooked long grain white rice, warm
1 1/2 cups diced tomato, seeds discarded,
1/3 cup chopped fresh parsley
1/3 cup sliced green onions, white and green parts
1 t. minced garlic
Kosher salt
pepper
1/2 cup sour cream
1 cup grated white Cheddar cheese
4 10-11" flour tortillas

Heat the black-eyed peas in a large nonreactive saucepan over med. heat. Add the rice, tomatoes, parsley, green onions, and garlic. Season with kosher salt and pepper to taste. Cook over low heat until warm, 2-3 minutes. Stir to combine thoroughly.
Divide the sour cream among the tortillas and spread evenly over each tortilla, leaving at least a 1" border around the edge. Sprinkle the cheese evenly over the sour cream. Divide the black-eyed pea mixture among the tortillas and wrap. Serves 4

Instant Russian Tea
Donna Ericson

1 c. instant tea powder
2 c. tang
1 3-oz pkg imitation lemonade mix
1-1/2 c. sugar
½ tsp ground cloves
½ tsp cinnamon

Gently mix all ingredients in medium sized bowl. Spoon into screw top jar. When ready to serve, use approximately 3 spoonfuls in boiling water.

SOUPS

Summer Corn Chowder
Dona Ericson

2 T. olive oil
1/2 cup (1/4" diced) green
2 T. unsalted butter
green bell pepper
1 large onion, 1/4" diced
salt to taste
3 T. flour
1/4 t. pepper

5 cups veg. broth
1 cup 1/2 & 1/2
2 russet potatoes, 1/4" dice
2 plum tomatoes, 1/4" diced,
4 cups corn kernels
1/2 cup (1/4" diced) red bell pepper
1/2 cup thinly slivered fresh basil, for garnish

1. Place the oil and butter in a pot over low heat. Add the diced onion and wilt for about 10 minutes. Sprinkle the flour over the onion; cook, stirring, for an additional 3-5 minutes.
2. Add the broth and potatoes; bring to a boil. Reduce the heat to medium and cook, partially covered, for 10 minutes or until
the potatoes are tender, stirring occasionally.
3. Add the corn, red and green bell peppers, salt, pepper and 1/2 & 1/2; cook over low heat for 8 minutes, stirring occasionally.
4. Ladle 2 cups of soup into each bowl. Before serving, place 1 T. of diced tomatoes in the center of each and top generously with slivered basil. Serve immediately.

Onion Soup from Denmark
Donna Ericson

4 onions
2 T. butter
4 cups boiling water
8 beef bouillon cubes
salt and pepper

4 slices toast
butter
4 slices cheese

Peel and roughly chop the onions. Melt the butter in a pot. Saute the onions until golden and transparent. Add the boiling water and the bouillon cubes. Bring the soup to a boil and let it simmer for half an hour. Add salt and pepper to taste.

Spread butter on the bread and lay the cheese on top. Grill for a few minutes in a preheated oven.

Serve the soup in bowls with the cheese bread floating on top.

Corny Chowder
Donna Ericson

Saute in large pot until soft:
1 T. olive oil
1 1/2 cups chopped onion
1 T. dry sherry

Add, bring to boil and simmer until vegetables are tender:
1 cup celery, chopped
1 cup carrots, sliced
2 cups new potatoes, cubed
1 cup chicken broth
1 bay leaf
Simmer 5 minutes and remove bay leaf

Add:
1 cup milk
1 1/2 cups frozen, thawed, corn kernels

Add dollop of sour cream to each serving:

Creamy Artichoke Soup
Donna Ericson

1/2 cup chopped onion
2 T. butter
1 14oz. can artichoke hearts, save liquid and finely chop
  artichokes
1/4 t. oregano

1/4 t. ginger
1/2 cup Chardonay wine
1 dash white pepper to taste
2 T. flour
1 cup chicken stock
2 cups milk

Saute onion in butter until soft. Add chopped artichokes, flour and seasonings to onion, blend well. Slowly add chicken stock, wine, artichoke liquid and milk. Stir until smooth and slightly thickened. Serve hot or cold. Garnish cold with lime slices, hot with shredded parmesan.

Chicken and Dumplings Soup
Donna Ericson

1 whole large chicken
1 cup chopped carrots
1 cup chopped celery
1 cup chopped onions
2 T. dried parsley
salt and pepper

In a deep stock pot add all ingredients and enough water to cover chicken. Cook several hours. Remove chicken and de-bone it. Transfer the chicken meat, broth and vegetables to a large roasting pan, bring to a boil. Drop dumplings in by the large spoonful. Cover and cook 20 minutes. Serve immediately.

Dumplings:
2 cups Bisquick
2/3 cup milk
Mix until soft dough forms.

Chili
Donna Ericson (quilter Robin Stilwell)

2# ground beef
1 cup water
1 16 oz. can pureed tomatoes
1 onion, finely chopped
1 t. garlic powder
1 t. Tabasco
1/4 cup chili powder
1 t. ground oregano
2 t. ground cumin
1 1/2 t. salt
12 oz. beer
1 4 oz. can chopped green chilies
1 can pinto beans

Brown met and drain. Add water, pureed tomatoes, onion and garlic powder. Bring to boil, reduce heat and simmer, covered for 30 minutes, stirring occasionally. Add remaining ingredients. Stir well. Simmer uncovered for 30 minutes, then covered for 30 minutes.

(*Optional- if thicker chili is desired, stir in smooth paste of flour and water. Cook several minutes longer to thicken.)

Mashed Potato Soup
Donna Ericson

6-8 medium potatoes, peeled and boiled
1/2# bacon, cut into small pieces and fried
1 cup med. cheddar cheese, grated
2 green onions, chopped
1/2 cup sour cream
milk

Mash potatoes with milk and sour cream. Mash to thin consistency, but not runny. Spoon into flat soup bowls, garnish with bacon, onion and cheese.

Benson's Mexican Soup
Devvi Morgan

2 cans chicken broth
1 can Mexicorn, undrained
salsa (medium) to taste
1 can black beans, rinsed with cold water & drained

Heat. Pour over tortilla chips and grated cheddar cheese.

Baked Potato Soup
Donna Ericson

5 - 6 large potatoes, baked, cooled, peeled and diced
2 cans chicken broth
1/2 lb. bacon, set aside 2 strips, cook and crumble the rest for garnish
1 medium onion, peeled and diced
1/2 stick butter

1 cup milk and 1 sm. carton cream
salt and pepper to taste
Additional garnish - opt.
  sour cream
  grated cheddar
  chopped green onion

In large soup pan, melt butter and saute onions. Add potatoes, 1/2 t. salt and bacon strips. Stir and add chicken broth. Bring to a boil and continue to boil till potatoes begin to break down. Then remove from heat. Remove bacon and discard. With a potato masher or electric mixer, mash potatoes until they are like very lumpy mashed potatoes. Add milk and cream then salt and pepper to taste. Serve with dollup of sour cream, grated cheese, crumbled bacon, green onion.

Vegetable Beef Soup
Lyn Olsen

Cut beef roast into chunks, flour and brown with salt and pepper, garlic if desired, until golden brown in grease in big pot. Then add 1 small can tomato sauce and water, then simmer covered for several hours. Then add peeled potatoes cut into cubes into the soup about half an hour before serving (do not cook potatoes too long so they are not mushy but still slightly firm). About 15 minutes before serving add canned peas or beans.

Growing up, Butte was full of local home-cooking restaurants and cafes, and 4B's was one of those places where everyone went whether for breakfast where you would always find Milo or after the bars closed at 2 am. Other outstanding restaurants and cafes includes Lydia's fine dining where you got several courses during your dinner beginning with the best appetizers such as raviolis which you filled up on and then took your meal home.

Terri's and Fred and Millie's were home-cooking cafés down on the flats by the Saddle Club. Terri's served some of the best Butte pasties with gravy, but for Fred and Millie's I walked a lot more than a mile almost every day during the summer; in fact, I walked 6 miles from my neighborhood starting up by the Big M hill just blocks down from the highly distinctive white Immaculate Conception Church overlooking all of Butte and the distant Highland mountains whereby I could always judge when winter was approaching by the snow collected on them. From there, I walked down to the Saddle Club so that I could muck out the manured-filled stalls of my aunt's horses. For all of that, my aunt would buy me pay me with French fries from Fred and Millie's; in those days, it was a rare treat to eat out.

Beef Stew with Dumplings
Myrna Miller
One of mom's best for dinner – loved it!

Cut roast into large chunks, flour and brown in grease with salt and pepper as well as garlic. When done, add flour mixture (several tablespoons flour mixed with water so no lumps – can strain), stir the entire time so gravy is made. Keep adding water to be sure it doesn't clump but becomes slightly thickened. Add several bay leaves and cook for several hours covered on simmer – make sure there is enough water so nothing lumps up. About 30 minutes before eating add potatoes cut into large chunks and carrots cut into pieces and cook until tender. Before serving prepare dumplings by using recipe on Bisquick which includes milk and Bisquick until doughy, then dump by spoonful onto stew which is cooking on low. Cover for 10 minutes, then take cover off and cook another 10 minutes. **My quicker version of Beef Stew:** Brown hamburger with onion, salt and pepper, garlic if you want; add one can cream of mushroom soup and several bay leaves, add water and cook on low for several hours. About 30 minutes before serving add shredded potatoes and carrots. Cook until tender and serve. Can skip bay leaves and add sour cream before serving to make stroganoff.

Ham and Bean Soup
Myrna Miller

Put small bag of navy beans in bowel and cover with water that covers the beans with an extra 1 inch of water. Cover with a towel and let soak overnight. The next day, take the ham bone with meat on the bone from a previous ham dinner and place in big pot with enough water to cover it. Add onion, salt and pepper to taste. Cook on low for 5 hours. Add beans and their water and cook on low again for several hours.

Best 4B's Tomato Soup
Donna Ericson (best soup ever, too bad this NW chain has closed)

32 oz. can diced tomatoes
9 oz. can chicken broth, undiluted
1 oz. butter
2 T. sugar
1 T. chopped onion
pinch baking soda
2 cups 1/2 & ½

Mix everything together except for the cream and simmer for one hour. Heat cream in a double boiler. Add cream to tomato mixture.

CHAPTER 3 MAIN COURSE

Spaghetti Carbonara (eggless)
Donna Ericson

1# dry spaghetti
3/4 cup crumbled cooked bacon (about 12 strips)
1 cup frozen petite peas
2 1/2 cups heavy cream
1 cup freshly grated Parmesan cheese
1 T. chopped fresh Italian parsley
freshly ground black pepper

Bring a large pot of salted water to a rapid boil. Add the pasta and cook until al dente, 8 to 9 minutes. Meanwhile, in a large frying pan over med-high heat, heat the bacon pieces until they begin to sizzle. Add the peas and cream. Bring the sauce to a boil, reduce the heat slightly, and boil gently for about 8 minutes. Sprinkle in the Parmesan, stirring continuously to blend it in and thicken the sauce. Drain the pasta thoroughly and immediately toss it with the sauce in a mixing or serving bowl. Transfer to individual warm serving bowls, garnish with the chopped parsley and add black pepper to taste.

Creamed Tuna Fish on Toast
Myrna Miller

Though simple, one of our favorites as kids.

Make white sauce by melting several tablespoons of butter on medium heat. Then add several tablespoons of flour and stir constantly until thickened, at least several minutes. Add 1 c milk slowly, stirring constantly. Let thicken some and then add more milk and let it thicken. Continue this until the mixture is slightly thickened and cooked, approximately 2 to 3 cups of milk. Take off heat and add 2 drained cans of tuna fish and 6 or more hardboiled eggs. Make toast and put mixture on buttered toast.

Teriyaki Chicken
Lyn Olsen

Cook chicken pieces in light oil on stove top until done, then add the following ingredients: ½ c. pineapple juice, ¼ c. soy sauce, ¼ c. dry cooking sherry, 2 tablespoons brown sugar and ¼ tsp ground ginger. Cook and add water as necessary.

Linguine with Fresh Tomato-Olive Sauce
Donna Ericson

3 1/2 cups seeded and diced fresh plum tomatoes
1 t. minced garlic
1/2 cup pitted and chopped Kalamata olives
1/4 cup diced yellow pepper
1/2 cup plus 2 T. slivered fresh basil leaves
1/2 cup chopped green onions
1/4 cup extra-virgin olive oil
2 T. fresh lemon juice
salt and freshly ground pepper, to taste
1 # fresh or dried linguine
8 oz. fresh Mozzarella, cut into 1/2" cubes (optional)
Freshly grated Parmigiano-Reggiano

In a large bowl, combine tomatoes, garlic, olives, yellow pepper, 1/2 cup basil, green onions, olive oil, lemon juice, salt and pepper; stir to combine and let sauce stand at room temperature, stirring occasionally, about 30 minute. Fill a large pot two thirds full of water, bring to a boil, add salt and pasta, and cook according to package instructions; drain pasta. In a large bowl, combine pasta, tomato/olive sauce and fresh mozzarella, and toss to mix well. Divide among 4 individual bowls, and garnish with remaining 2 T. basil and the freshly grated Parmigiano-Reggiano. Serves 4.

Colorful Pasta with ham
Donna Ericson

16 oz. tricolor spiral pasta
1 1/2 cups cubed fully cooked ham
1 can (15 1/4 oz.) whole kernel corn, drained
1 1/2 cups (6 oz.) shredded cheddar cheese, divided
1 can (2.8 oz) french-fried onions, divided
1 can (14 1/2 oz.) canned chicken broth
1 can (10 3/4 oz.) cream of chicken soup, undiluted
1/2 cup milk
1/2 t. each celery salt, garlic powder and pepper

Cook pasta according to package directions; drain. In a large bowl, combine the pasta, ham, corn, 1 cup cheese and 3/4 cup onions. In another bowl, combine the broth, soup, milk and seasonings. Pour over pasta mixture; mix well. Pour into a greased 9x13" pan. Bake, uncovered, at 350 degrees for 30 minutes. Sprinkle with remaining cheese and onions. Bake 5 minutes longer or until heated through. Yield - 8 servings.

Gravy
Myrna Miller

Although my mom made this look simple to make, gravy really isn't, especially to get it right but my mom's gravy was the absolute best.

Brown meat and then either on the stove top or in the oven, cover and cook at a low temperature with water, perhaps dry onion soup mix for several hours. This recipe is also for turkey and any meat that produces a brown sauce of drippings. Remove the meat, and put the pan on the stove top at medium heat. Mix several tablespoons of flour with 2 cups of medium temperature water, mix well, shake, and a strainer can be used to be sure there are no lumps of flour. Slowly pour into the drippings as they are heating and stir. Add salt and pepper to taste. Continue to stir and let heat and to thicken. As gravy begins to thicken add a little more water, and continue to cook and stir, and repeat until the gravy has cooked for 5 or more minutes and is slightly thick.

A version of this for white gravy with chicken and pork chops is to put the drippings from cooking the meat into a fry pan. Add several tablespoons of flour to the drippings which should be more greasy and let cook for several minutes. It is important that the flour cooks in the grease/drippings enough so that it is cooked. Keep stirring the entire time and add salt and pepper to taste. Let the drippings and flour brown after several minutes, then slowly add milk, stirring constantly, let cook a little, then add more milk and repeat several times for more than 5 minutes until it has cooked enough and is now the consistency of thickness desired.

Tamale Pie with cornmeal biscuits
Donna Ericson

2# rump roast or chuck, chopped into 1/2 inch cubes
4 T. oil
Brown in batches and remove from pan.

In same pan saute 1 large onion, chopped, 2 large jalapeños chopped, 3 T. chili powder, 4 cloves garlic, chopped, 1 t. salt, 16 oz. can pinto beans, 1 can or jar pimento stuffed olives, chopped, 28 oz. crushed tomatoes, 10 oz. frozen corn, 1 1/2 cups water. Simmer for 20 minutes, then add meat and simmer uncovered until quite thick. Can be frozen at this stage.

Cornmeal drop biscuits:
Whisk: 1 cup flour, 1 c. cornmeal, 3 oz. sharp cheddar, grated, 1 1/2 T. sugar, 2 t. baking powder, 1/2 t. salt, 1/2 t. cumin, 1 med. jalapeño, chopped.

Whisk: 3/4 cup milk, 3 T. melted butter and 1 egg.

Add to above dry mixture and mix just to blend. Drop by large rounded T. onto hot tamale mixture. Bake at 400 degrees 10 minutes, then at 350 degrees for 30 minutes.

Taco Bake
Donna Ericson (quilter friend Carol K.)

Note: I am going to add 1 cup corn from now on.

1 # ground beef	8 oz. (2 c.) shell or elbow macaroni, cooked and drained
1 sm. chopped onion	
3/4 c. water	1 sm. can chopped chilies
1 pkg. Taco seasoning	2 c. shredded Cheddar, divided
1 - 15 oz. can tomato sauce	

Brown gr. beef and onion, drain. Add water, seasoning mix, tomato sauce. Simmer 20 minutes. Mix beef, macaroni and
1 3/4 c. cheese. Put into casserole. Sprinkle remaining cheese on top. Bake at 350 degrees 30 minutes.

One of my earliest and most enduring memories of Thanksgiving in Montana was waking up at 6 am to help my mom prepare the turkey and dressing. The heat would seep out into the room, leaving the windows fogged due to the contrast between the steam of the cooking turkey and the cold outside where the snow quietly fluttered down all day. Mirrored in companionship were my earliest memories of the poems we had to memorize in grade school; I still remember from second grade, one by James Russell Lowell (1787-1900):

THE SNOW had begun in the gloaming,
And busily all the night
Had been heaping field and highway
With a silence deep and white.
Every pine and fir and hemlock
Wore ermine too dear for an earl,
And the poorest twig on the elm-tree
Was ridged inch deep with pearl.
From sheds new-roofed with Carrara
Came Chanticleer's muffled crow,
The stiff rails softened to swan's-down,
And still fluttered down the snow.

Turkey Dressing
Myrna Miller

The day before put out several loaves of bread on the countertop (take out of bag) and spread them so they are not on top of each other. Let sit all night and get hard. Next morning cut into medium size squares.

Put a stick of butter (or double if you want lots of dressing) in a large fry pan and melt over medium heat. As it is melting, add chopped celery and onions and cook until tender. Add lots of sage, like several large teaspoons, salt and pepper.

Pour the butter mixture over the bread in a large bowl and mix. Add milk slowly until desired consistency, that is slightly wet but not gooey and so bread maintains some consistency and does not become a clump.

Make sure turkey was thawed. Stuff into turkey by neck area and big cavity. Tie up legs, salt and pepper turkey and put in roaster with lid into 350 oven as directed by weight on turkey package.

Mexican Fiesta Pie
Donna Ericson

1/2# ground beef
1/4 cup chopped onion
2 t. chili powder
8 oz. cream cheese, cubed

4 oz. can chopped chilies, drained
1/2 cup pitted ripe olives
2 eggs, beaten

Brown meat; drain; add onions, cook till tender. Stir in chili powder. Add cream cheese, chilies, olives and eggs, mix well. Set aside.

3/4 cup flour
1/3 cup milk
2 eggs, beaten

1 T. cornmeal
1 cup chopped tomato
1 cup (4 oz.) shredded cheddar

Combine flour, milk and eggs and beat until smooth. Pour into greased 10 inch pie plate. Sprinkle with cornmeal. Spoon meat mixture over batter to within 1/2 inch of outer edge of pan. Bake at 400 degrees 35 - 40 minutes or till golden brown. Top with tomatoes and cheese, continue baking 5 minutes.

Chili Mac Ole
Donna Ericson
(I found the tomatoes with chilies added were too spicy, so I changed it to just plain tomatoes)

Ingredients:
2 cups elbow macaroni, uncooked
1 15 oz. can Hormel Chili No Beans
1 10 oz. can diced tomatoes, no chilies added
1/2 med. green pepper, chopped
3 green onions, sliced
dash salt
3/4 c. shredded American or Cheddar cheese

Cook macaroni, drain. In medium saucepan heat remaining ingredients (reserving 1/4 cup cheese) until cheese melts, stirring frequently. Arrange macaroni on platter; pour chili mixture over; top with remaining cheese. Garnish as desired. Refrigerate leftovers. 6 servings.
If casserole is desired; combine cooked macaroni and remaining ingredients. Pour into a 2-quart baking dish. Bake at 350 degrees 25 minutes

Cornbread Skillet Casserole
Donna Ericson (quilter friend Carol E.)

1# lean ground beef
1/4 cup veg. oil
2 eggs, beaten
2 cups shredded cheddar cheese
1 cup self-rising corn meal
1 large onion, chopped
1 can (16oz.) cream style corn
2-4 jalepeno peppers, seeded and chopped
1 cup milk

Crumble ground beef into a large skillet and brown evenly; drain. Stir eggs, corn meal, cream style corn, milk and oil together. Pour 1/2 batter into greased 10 1/2" cast iron skillet or 10 inch deep dish pie plate. Top evenly with browned ground beef followed by the cheese, onion and peppers. Pour remaining batter over the top. Bake in preheated 350 degree oven 45-55 minutes. Let stand 5-10 minutes before cutting into wedges to serve. Makes 6-8 servings.

Corn Casserole
Donna Ericson (card playing and quilting friend Carol Enrooth)
Excellent

1/2 of a medium onion, chopped	1 can creamed corn
1/2 of a green pepper, chopped	1 box Jiffy corn muffin mix
1 stick butter	2 eggs
1 can corn	1/2 - 3/4 cup cheese

Saute onion and pepper in butter, then mix all ingredients together. Pour into 9x13" pan and bake at 350 degrees 1/2 hour or until set. Let stand 5 minutes or more before serving.

Chicken Tamale Pie
Donna Ericson (from quilter Nancy Sprague)
DELICIOUS!

Nancy served sour cream, chopped green onions and shredded cheddar to put on top of this.

Red Sauce:
- 2 T. + 1 1/2 t. chili powder
- 3 T. sugar
- 1 cup + 2 T. flour
- 1 T. + 1 1/2 t. paprika
- 1/4 t. oregano
- 1 3/4 t. salt
- 1/4 t. cumin
- 1 1/2 t. garlic powder
- 2 T. chicken stock base
- 5 cups water
- 1/2 cup + 1 1/2 t. butter
- 12 oz. tomato paste

6 whole chicken breasts or 6-7# turkey breast, cooked, cut up in chunks. Combine dry ingredients and blend with spoon to remove lumps. Add some of the water and blend to a smooth paste. Add remaining water, butter and tomato paste. Cook slowly, stirring constantly until thick (like a thick white sauce...takes about 15 minutes). Add cooked chicken or turkey. Stir to coat. Set aside.

Corn Meal:
- 2 1/2 cups cornmeal
- 1 T. + 3/4 t. salt
- 1 1/4 cup flour
- 10 cups water
- 1/2 t. + 1/8 t. pepper
- 10 T. butter
- 2 T. + 1 1/2 t. chicken stock base

Combine dry ingredients and blend with spoon to remove lumps. Add water and butter. Cook slowly, stirring constantly until water and butter are absorbed (like hot cereal.....takes about 15 minutes). Pour 1/2 of cornmeal into greased oblong pan. Top with red sauce. Top with remaining cornmeal. Bake at 350 degrees for 1 hour. This recipe is enough to fill two 9x13" pans or 1 large oblong pan comparable in size to 2 - 9x13 pans. Can be frozen to bake another time.

Mexican Stuffed Shells
Devvi Morgan

12 pasta stuffing shells, cooked and drained,
1# ground beef
1 jar (12 oz.) mild picante sauce
1/2 c. water

1 can (8 oz) tomato sauce
1 can (4 oz) chopped green chilies, drained
1 c. (4 oz). shredded Monterey Jack Cheese
1 can (2.8 oz.) Durkee French Fried Onions

Brown ground beef; drain. Combine picante sauce, water and tomato sauce; stir 1/2 cup into ground beef along with chilies, 1/2 cup cheese and 1/2 can French Fried Onions; mix well. Pour half of remaining sauce mixture on bottom of 10" round or 8x12" baking dish. Stuff cooked shells with ground beef mixture. Arrange shells in baking dish; pour remaining sauce over shells. Bake, covered, at 350 degrees for 30 minutes. Top with remaining cheese and onions; bake, uncovered, 5 minutes longer.

We weren't able to find the stuffing shells, so we used Manicotti and it worked fine. I sometimes substitute macaroni (this is a lot easier), too.

MAIN DISHES

Beef Stroganoff
Lyn Olsen

Brown hamburger meat or any other meat, chopped or ground. Pour grease off. Add one can of mushroom soup, salt, and pepper to taste. Cover and simmer for ½ to 1 hour. Just before serving add sour cream to taste.

Chop Suey
Myrna Miller

Take leftover pork roast, cut into cubes, brown and fry until golden brown in pan with onions and celery on stove with grease from roast. Then add flour mixture composed of several tablespoons of flour and water mixed together without lumps (can strain if necessary) to the meat and add water to make sure it does not clump while stirring constantly, making a gravy. When gravy is good to your taste, add soy sauce to taste. Pour this mixture into already cooked rice so that the gravy is able to cover all of the rice.

Savory Pot Roast
Donna Ericson
Everyone just loves this!

5# boneless chuck pot roast or similar pot roast	1/4 c. wine vinegar
6 T. margarine	2 bay leaves, 4 sprigs parsley, 1 t. whole black pepper corns
1-1/2 c. chopped onion	1 T. anchovy paste (in dairy counter)
2 cloves crushed garlic	2 T. honey or corn syrup
1/3 c. flour	2 cans beef broth.

Brown roast, set aside. Pre-heat oven to 325 degrees. Add onion and garlic to drippings. Cook 5 minutes. Remove from heat, stir in flour until smooth. Add vinegar, anchovy paste, honey and broth. Tie bay leaves, parsley and peppers in cheese cloth bag. Add to above. Bring to boiling. Add roast. Cover and cook in oven 3 to 3-1/2 hours.

NOTE: This works very well in a crockpot (low-all day).

Shredded BBQ Beef
Donna Ericson

1 4# boneless rump roast, remove as much fat as possible (see note below)
3 T. oil

1 large onion, chopped	2 T. prepared mustard
1 cup ketchup	2 T. molasses
1 cup beef broth	2 T. lemon juice
2/3 cup chili sauce	1 t. salt
1/4 cup vinegar	1/8 t. pepper
1/4 cup packed brown sugar	12-16 Kaiser rolls or hamburger buns
3 T. worchestershire sauce	

In a Dutch oven, brown roast on all sides in 1 T. oil. Meanwhile, in a large saucepan, saute onion in remaining oil until tender. Add remaining ingredients, except rolls; bring to a boil. Reduce heat; simmer, uncovered, for 15 minutes, stirring occasionally. Pour over roast. Cover and bake at 325 for 2 hours; turn the roast over and bake for 2 more hours or until meat is very tender. Remove roast; shred with fork and return to sauce. Serve on rolls.

Note: I made this 2/25/03 using a boneless chuck roast. It was quite tough, so from now on, I am going to use a rump roast and cook it in a crock pot.

My grandmother Lil was a perfectionist, but truthfully she was always the best at everything she did. I remember she sewed an entire white velvet wedding dress by hand. Like a true Montanan, she always took good care of her family and neighbors, cooking huge feasts that left you wanting more even after your belly hurt from being stuffed.

Fourth of July was always particularly memorable, filled with the warmth of her cinnamon rolls fresh out of the oven and breakfasts following the infamous parade.

Growing up in Butte, I remember other incidences that demonstrated her perfectionistic behavior. One time, but only one time, my aunt had somehow convinced my grandmother to go out for dinner. Before going to the Ponderosa (a very good steakhouse on Harrison Avenue across from Fred and Millie's), my aunt warned me that grandmother might be difficult. Apprehensive, I sat expectantly at dinner waiting, and it didn't take long; Soon after the food began arriving, the criticism began flying and shortly thereafter my grandmother walked out, having barely touched her food. Her only comment repeated over and over was that she could have made the food so much better and that it would never have cost so much...that was the only and last time she went out to eat.

Another incident was when the Three Sisters convinced their mom to let them hire a housekeeper – mistake number 2 for those sisters who you would have thought knew better. My grandmother was up all night cleaning house before the housekeeper came....because she certainly did not want anyone to think that she was not a great housekeeper. That was the last time for that too. My grandmother was the best at whatever she did.

Chicken Honey Nut Stir-Fry
Donna Ericson
Very Good

1 # boneless chicken breasts
2 T. oil, divided
3/4 cup orange juice
2 large carrots, cut diagonally
1/3 cup honey
2 stalks celery, "   "

3 T. soy sauce
1/2 cup cashews or peanuts
1 T. cornstarch
Hot rice
1/4 t. ground ginger (I used grated fresh ginger)

I added some thin strips of red, green and yellow peppers, which I had roasted and peeled.

Cut chicken into thin strips and set aside. In a small bowl, combine orange juice, honey, soy sauce, cornstarch and ginger; mix well. Heat 1 T. oil in a large skillet over medium heat. Add carrots and celery; stir-fry about 3 minutes. Remove vegetables and set aside. Pour remaining oil into skillet. Add chicken; stir-fry about 3 minutes. Return vegetables to skillet; add sauce mixture and nuts. Cook and stir over medium-high heat until sauce is thickened. Serve over hot rice. Makes 4 to 6 servings.

Coconut Shrimp Two With Red Curry Sauce
Donna Ericson

1/4 cup cornstarch
1 T. fresh mint, chopped
3 egg whites
2 T. oil
2 cups unsweet coconut flakes
2 T. Thai red curry paste*

1 1/2# jumbo shrimp, peel, leave tails on
1 cup unsweet coconut milk*
1 lime, juiced
1 green onion, sliced
peanut or canola oil for frying

*Available in the Asian or ethnic food aisle of supermarket
In a small bowl, mix the cornstarch, egg white and some salt and pepper until foamy. Spread the coconut in a pie plate. Dredge the shrimp in the egg white mixture and shake off excess. Press the shrimp into the coconut flakes, repeating on other side.

Shallow fry the shrimp in batches until the coconut is golden brown, about 2 to 3 minutes. Using tongs or a slotted spoon, remove the shrimp to paper towels to drain. Arrnge the shrimp on a platter and serve immediately with red curry sauce and garnish with green onions and mint.

To make the red curry sauce, place a small pot over med. heat and coat with oil. Stir the red curry paste into the pan and cook until aromatic. Slowly pour in the coconut milk and continue to stir to incorporate. Add the lime juice and one of the halves of the squeezed lime for additional flavor and cook for 5 to 10 minutes to thicken. Pour the sauce into a serving bowl and serve with the shrimp.

Crab Cakes
Donna Ericson

Mix together 1 T. Worcestershire
1 dash hot sauce
1 egg, beaten
1 T. Dijon mustard
1/2 cup mayonnaise

Stir. Crush 20 saltine crackers by hand and add to above mixture, blending well. Add 1# crab meat (canned Jumbo lump, canned) Shape into cakes. Can be frozen at this stage. Defrost in fridge. Brown on both sides in hot oil.

German Engineering
Donna Ericson

3 T. sherry vinegar
2 T. honey mustard
2 t. caraway seeds
1 1/2 t. celery salt
pepper
1/4 cup + 2 t. olive oil
1# small red potatoes, cut into 1" cubes (do not peel)
Kosher salt
1 cup diced onion
1 cup diced green bell pepper, seeds and ribs discarded
1# kielbasa sausage, cut in half lengthwise and sliced into 1/4" half circles
4 10-11" flour tortillas

Combine the vinegar, mustard, caraway seeds, celery salt, and 1/4 t. pepper in a small bowl. Gradually whisk in 1/4 cup of the olive oil. Set aside.

Place the potatoes in a large saucepan and cover with water. Add 1 T. kosher salt and bring to a boil over high heat. Reduce heat and simmer until potatoes are tender when pierced with a fork, about 30 minutes. Remove from heat, drain and return the potatoes to the sauce pan. Using a handheld masher or a large fork, mash into a coarse mixture. Add the vinegar mixture and mix well.

Heat the remaining 2 t. olive oil in a large nonstick skillet over med. heat. Add the onion, bell pepper, 1/2 t. kosher salt and 1/4 t. pepper. Cook until onions and peppers become tender and start to brown, 5-7 minutes. Add the onions and peppers to the mashed potatoes and stir to combine. Wipe the skillet clean with a paper towel and return the skillet to the stove. Heat the skillet over high heat and add the kielbasa. Cook until brown, about 5-7 minutes. Add the potato mixture and mix well. Cook until warm. Divide among the tortillas and wrap.

Yum-a-Setta
Donna Ericson

The men really love this recipe!

2 # hamburger	1 can tomato soup - undiluted
salt & pepper to taste	1 can cream of chicken soup, undiluted
1/4 c. brown sugar	16 oz. noodles
1/4 onion, chopped	8 oz. Cheddar Cheese

Brown hamburger with salt, pepper, brown sugar and onion. Add tomato soup. Cook noodles, drain. Add chicken soup to noodles. Layer hamburger, cheese, noodles and cheese. Bake at 350 degrees for 30 minutes.

Italian Revolution
Donna Ericson

4 uncooked bacon slices, diced	3/4 cup dry white wine
1 1/4# boneless skinless chicken breasts, cut into 1/4" strips	1/2 cup heavy cream
	1/8 t. ground nutmeg
Kosher salt	1 cup green peas
Pepper	1 cup grated Swiss cheese
1 T. olive oil	1 1/2 cups warm cooked orzo
1 cup diced onion	4 10-11" flour tortillas
1 t. flour	

Heat a large nonstick skillet over med. heat. Add the bacon and cook until crispy and brown, about 5 minutes, stirring occasionally. Transfer the bacon to a paper towel-lined plate using a slotted spoon.

Return the skillet to the stove and heat over high heat. Add the chicken and season with 1 t. kosher salt and 1/4 t. pepper. Cook until chicken is cooked through, 4-6 minutes, turning to brown all sides. Remove from heat and transfer the chicken to a large bowl using a slotted spoon. Add the bacon and gently stir to combine.

Wipe the skillet clean with a paper towel to remove all meat residue and return the skillet to the stove. Add the olive oil and heat over medium heat. Add the onion, flour, 1/2 t. kosher salt, and 1/4 t. pepper. Cook until the onions become soft, about 10 minutes. Add the wine and cream and bring to a boil. Cook until mixture becomes thick, 4 to 5 minutes. Add the nutmeg and peas; cook 1 minute. Add the chicken mixture, cheese, and orzo and stir to combine thoroughly. Divide among the tortillas and wrap. Serves 4.

My mom moved to Butte when I was in the sixth grade so that we could be near her mom and sisters to help her raise her six kids. Times were tough as my mom worked several minimum wage jobs just to put a roof over our head and food on our table which was sometimes scarce. Powdered milk was a mainstay for us as bad as it tasted.

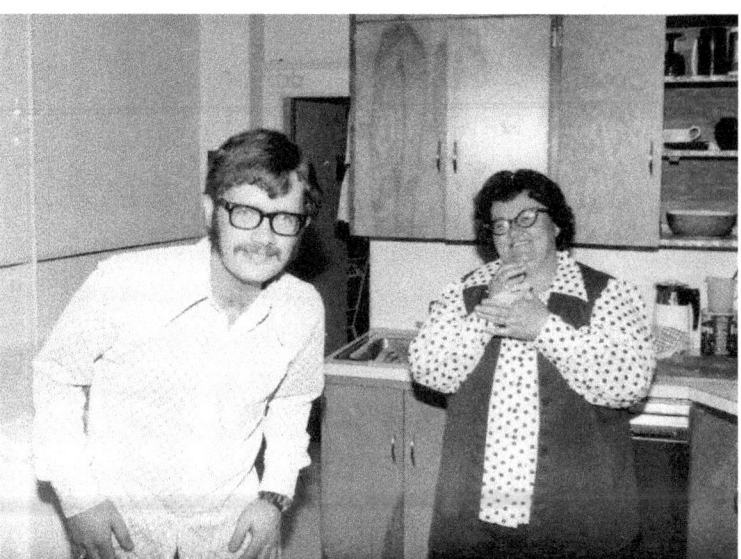

It was during that time in the 70's that my mom was given a freezer full of frozen chickens (in the background behind my brother) which was a treat for us, well was....it is hard to eat chicken for lunch and dinner every day for months. My grandmother, the superb cook, tried to ameliorate the situation by cooking chicken in more ways than one might have thought possible, and Chicken Tetrazinni as one of those; I did not eat chicken after this for many years.

Chicken Tetrazinni
Lilian Beaulieu

6 T. butter
3 T. olive oil
1/2# fresh mushrooms, sliced
4 T. flour
1/8 t. nutmeg
3 cups cubed, cooked turkey

1/2# spaghetti
2 cups chicken broth
1 c. heavy cream or lo fat milk
2 T. dry sherry
3/4 cup grated Parmesan
1/4 cup bread crumbs

Heat 4 T. butter and oil in saucepan, add mushrooms, saute 5 minutes.
Remove mushrooms and reserve. Add flour to pan, stir to form a rue. Cook until bubbly, add broth and cook until thick. Remove from heat. Add cream, sherry, cheese and nutmeg. Stir until cheese melts. Add turkey and mushrooms. Stir well. Combine with spaghetti and pour into 9x13 baking dish. Melt 2 T. butter and combine with bread crumbs, sprinkle over dish.
Bake 25-30 minutes at 375 degrees.

Tropical Chicken
Donna Ericson

1/2 small onion, thinly sliced and separated into rings
2 boneless, skinless chicken breasts
1 8-ounce can pineapple chunks, drained
1/2 medium red bell pepper, cut into strips
3 T. teriyaki sauce
2 T. packed brown sugar
1/2 t. grated fresh ginger
2 cups hot cooked rice

Preheat oven to 450 degrees or grill to medium-high. Divide onion and center on 2 12x18-inch sheets of heavy-duty aluminum foil. Top with chicken, pineapple and red pepper. Combine teriyaki sauce, brown sugar and ginger, spoon over chicken and vegetables.

Bring up foil sides. Double fold top and ends to seal packet, leaving room for heat circulation inside. Repeat to make another packet.

Bake 16 to 18 minutes on a cookie sheet in oven or grill 13 to 15 minutes in covered grill. Serve over rice with additional teriyaki sauce, if desired. Serves two.

Teriyaki Meat Strips
Donna Ericson (from best friend Betty Maki)

Marinade:
1/2 cup soy sauce
1 t. ground ginger
2 T. minced onion
1/4 Sake or dry white wine or vermouth or beer
1 clove garlic, minced
1 T. sugar

Combine above in large bowl.
2 T. oil
16 oz. can bean sprouts
6 oz. can water chestnuts
1 to 3 cups mushrooms, opt
2 to 2 1/2# round or flank steak cut in thin strips 1 to 2 cups celery, cut diagonally

Place meat in marinade for 2 to 3 hours at room temp. or overnite in refrigerator. Drain meat thoroughly. Heat veg. oil in wok, preheated to 370 degrees.

Place 1/2 of steak in wok and stir fry for 2 min. Push up side and stir fry rest of the meat. Push up side and stir fry each veg. for 1 1/2 min. Lower heat and combine all ingredients. Serve over rice or noodles.

Cheesy Southwestern Meatloaf
Donna Ericson

1 cup prepared salsa, med
3 T. brown sugar
4 (6 inch) corn tortillas
1 1/2# ground chuck
1/2# ground pork
1/2 cup sour cream
3 large eggs
1 (4 oz.) can chopped green chilies
3/4 cup chopped scallions
1/4 cup minced fresh cilantro
1 T. chili powder
1 t. cumin
1 t. salt
1/2 t. pepper
1 cup grated pepper Jack cheese

1. Adjust oven rack to middle position and heat oven to 350 degrees. Line rimmed baking sheet with foil.
2. Combine salsa and brown sugar in small saucepan and set aside.
3. Tear tortillas into small pieces, grind in food processor or blender until they resemble cornmeal and transfer to large bowl. Add beef, pork, sour cream, eggs, chilies, scallions, cilantro, chili powder, cumin, salt and pepper and mix with fork until evenly blended. Turn mixture onto foil-lined baking sheet and using moistened hands, pat into 9x5 inch loaf shape. Brush with 1/3 cup salsa mixture.
4. Bake for 40 minutes. Scatter cheese on top and continue baking until center of loaf registers 160 degrees on instant-read thermometer, about 30 minutes. Set aside to cool slightly.

5. While meatloaf cools, simmer remaining salsa mixture over medium-high heat until thickened, 3 to 5 minutes. Slice meatloaf and serve with salsa mixture passed separately at table.

Chicken Marsala
Donna Ericson

3 T. flour
1/2 t. pepper
4 T. butter
1 T. veg. oil
1/2 cup chopped onion
1/2# mushrooms, sliced

3 T. dry marsala
2/3 cup beef stock,
salt to taste

4 skinless, boneless chicken breast halves, pounded to 1/4 inch

Mix flour and pepper in a shallow dish. Dredge chicken in flour mixture to coat; shake off excess. In a large fry pan, heat 2 T. of the butter in oil over med. heat. Add chicken and cook until lightly browned, about 3 minutes a side. Remove and keep warm. Add onion and garlic and saute until onion is tender. Add mushrooms and cook until they are lightly browned, 3-5 minutes. Return chicken to pan, stir in Marsala and beef stock. Bring to a boil, reduce heat, and simmer until liquid reduces by 1/3. Whisk in remaining butter. Season with salt and additional pepper to taste. Serve with buttered parsleyed noodles.

Mom's Meatloaf

Myrna Miller

Mix 3 pounds of hamburger with 1 pound of sausage (can substitute any other ground meat such as turkey but will not be as moist due to less grease). Add salt and pepper as well as cut onions if desired. In separate bowl, beat a couple of eggs with milk and add about 8 shakes of Worchestshire Sauce and mix well. Add to meat mixture. Add several cups of oatmeal intermittently with more milk and mix well until mixture is firm but very moist. Place in loaf pans and shape into loafs. Cook at 350 degrees until no pink in the middle.

Canelloni
Meat filling
Donna Ericson

8 oz. pkg. canelloni

Meat Filling:
4 T. olive oil
1 med. chopped onion
1 1/2 # ground beef
2 T. chopped parsley
salt and pepper to taste

2 eggs, slightly beaten
1/4 # mozzarella, diced
1/4# Swiss, grated
1 cup bread crumbs
2/3 cup milk

Cook 8 canelloni in 6 quarts of boiling water. Cook 5 minutes only. Remove carefully with strainer spoon. Run cold water over shells until cool enuf to handle.

Meat filling: Saute onion in oil. Add beef and season while meat cooks. When well browned, remove from heat and let cool. Mix in eggs, cheeses, bread crumbs and milk. Fill canelloni using a butter knife, then refrigerate until ready to use. When ready to bake, cover bottom of baking dish with spaghetti sauce. Lay cannelloni in side by side and cover with sauce. Cover with foil, crimping edges to seal. Bake @ 400 degrees for 40 minutes. Remove foil and bake another 10 minutes. Serves 8.

Simple filling with ricotta
1 - 16oz. ricotta cheese
1 1/2 cups grated Parmesan

3 eggs
salt and pepper to taste
1/2 cup chopped parsley

Blend all together. Fill shells that have been cooked and continue as above.

Quick Chicken Cordon Bleu
Lyn Olsen

Take leftover chicken and cut into thick strips. Cover with sliced him and mozzarella cheese. Season with salt and pepper and garlic if desired. Place in oven at 350 degrees and bake until golden brown.

Beef Brisket
Donna Ericson (quilter Carol E.)

3 or 4# beef brisket

Put meat in pan uncovered. Dump a package of dry onion soup mix on it and bake 1 hour at 325 degrees. Mix 1 can Coke, Pepsi or Tab (not diet) and 1/2 cup catsup together and pour over meat. Put lid on and bake at 275 degrees for 2 1/2 hours. Chill overnight, slice thin, put back in juice and heat up. Juice is good over rice or potatoes. Also makes excellent French dip sandwiches. (Slice on an angle).

Note: After cooking in the oven for 1 hour, it can be finished in a crock pot.

Barbequed Meat Balls
Todd's Favorite
Donna Ericson

1 can onion soup
1 can tomato soup
2 T. cornstarch
dash garlic powder
1/4 cup vinegar
1/4 cup brown sugar
1 T. Worcestershire

dash of Tabasco, opt.

Mix together.

Blend 1# ground beef, 1/2# bulk sausage, 1/2 cup soft bread crumbs, 1 egg.

Shape into meat balls. Brown and add sauce mixture and cook over low heat 20 minutes. Serve over rice. Brown meatballs in barbeque on hi 14 min. Use jelly roll pan and rack.

Fried Chicken

Myrna Miller

Flour cut chicken and put into hot grease. Brown on both sides on medium high heat, then put in an pan big enough to fit all of the chicken. Put a little water in the bottom and put a lid on. Bake at 250 for an hour or two unlikely flaky and moist.

For chicken gravy, put a couple of tablespoons of flour into the browned drippings from the chicken and on medium heat stir and brown the flour as well (can remove grease it too much grease). Cook for several minutes, then add about ½ to 1 cup of milk, stirring constantly. Let thicken slightly, then add more milk. Continue until enough gravy and a semi-thickened consistency. Add salt and pepper as desired. Pour gravy over potatoes and chicken.

Fried chicken and spaghetti were always an essential part of any great picnic in Butte, as well as swimming in the beautiful lakes of Montana. Although the swimming season was short in Butte, the lakes (such as this 1956 picture of us at Hauser Lake) and rivers were plentiful and only 10 minutes from town. My mom's fried chicken with white gravy was also our traditional meal every Sunday right before the Ed Sullivan Show. I remember one Ed Sullivan show in particular when at the age of 8 I had no idea why anyone got excited about a bunch of beetles and I couldn't imagine what talent they could have.

BBQ Beef
Donna Ericson

1 1/2# ground beef
1 onion, chopped
1/2 t. salt
1/2 t. pepper
14 oz. bottle ketchup
1 T. prepared mustard
1 T. vinegar
4 T. sugar' 1/2 cup water
1/4 t. paprika

Brown beef, onion and salt and pepper. Drain fat. Add all remaining ingredients and heat.

Baked Spaghetti
Donna Ericson (from Susan Carter - Water Therapy)

1 cup chopped onion
1 cup chopped green pepper
1 T. butter or margarine
1 can (28 oz.) tomatoes with liquid, cut up (I used S&W crushed tomatoes - Italian recipe w/basil and oregano. You don't have to cut these up.)
1 can (4 oz.) mushroom stems and pieces, drained (I used about 5 of the fresh small white ones, sliced)
1 can (2 1/4oz.) sliced ripe olives, drained
2 t. dried oregano (I only used 1 t.)
1# ground beef, browned and drained
12 oz. spaghetti, cooked and drained
2 cups (8 oz.) shredded cheddar cheese
1 can (10 3/4 oz.) condensed cream of mushroom soup, undiluted
1/4 cup water
1/4 cup grated Parmesan cheese

In large skillet, saute onion and green pepper in butter until tender. Add tomatoes, mushrooms, olives and oregano. Add ground beef if using. Simmer, uncovered, for 10 minutes. Place half of the spaghetti in greased 13x9x2" baking dish. Top with half of the vegetable mixture. Sprinkle with 1 cup of cheddar cheese. Repeat layers. Mix the soup and water until blended; pour over casserole. Sprinkle with Parmesan cheese. Bake, uncovered, at 350 degrees for 30-35 minutes or until heated through. Yield: 12 servings.

Note: Susan said she adds 1/2# pork sausage to the hamburger while browning it and then also adds about 1 cup of Mozzarella cheese besides the cheddar. I am going to try that next time.

Baked Beef Stew
Donna Ericson

1 can (14 1/2 oz.) diced tomatoes, undrained
1 cup water
3 T. quick-cooking tapioca
2 t. sugar
1 1/2 t. salt
1/2 t. pepper
2# lean beef stew meat, cut into 1-inch cubes
4 medium carrots, cut into 1-inch chunks
3 medium potatoes, peeled and quartered
2 celery ribs, cut into 3/4 inch chunks
1 medium onion, cut into chunks
1 slice bread, cubed

In a large bowl, combine the tomatoes, water, tapioca, sugar, salt and pepper. Add remaining ingredients; mix well. Pour into a greased 13 x 9 inch or 3-qt. baking dish. Cover and bake at 375 degrees for 1 3/4 to 2 hours or until meat and vegetables are tender. Serve in bowls.

Baked Chuck Roast
Donna Ericson

5# chuck roast
1 pkg. dry onion soup mix
2 - 12 oz. cans coke, Not Diet

Place roast in roasting pan. Sprinkle with soup. Pour coke over. Cover and seal tightly with foil. Bake at 250 degrees for 4 hours. Variation: Substitute 3-6 carrots, sliced, 1 can mushroom soup and dash garlic salt for coke.

Claudia's Mustard-crusted Pork Roast With Browned Potatoes
Devvi Morgan (Claudia is Sister-in-law)

1 (4-5#) boneless port loin roast
1/4 t. salt
1/4 t. pepper
1/2 cup coarse-grained mustard
8 garlic cloves, minced
3 T. chopped fresh rosemary
2 # new red potatoes
2 T. olive oil
1 T. chopped fresh rosemary
1/2 t. salt
1/12 t. pepper
Garnish: Fresh Rosemary sprigs

Place pork in a greased roasting pan. Rub with 1/4 t. each salt and pepper. Combine mustard and next 4 ingredients in a small bowl. Spread evenly over pork.

Peel a crosswise stripe around each potato with a veg. peeler, if desired. Cut each potato in half length-wise. Toss potatoes with 2 T. oil, 1 T. chopped rosemary, 1/2 t. salt and pepper. Add to roasting pan around pork. Insert meat therm. into the thickest part of the roast. Bake at 375 degrees for 1 hour to 1 1/4 hours or until therm. registers 160 degrees. Let stand 10 minutes. Transfer roast to a serving platter. Surround pork with potatoes. Garnish, if desired. 8 servings

Two of the most infamous foods from Butte are the porkchop sandwich and pasty – I have not found them equaled anywhere else.

The best porkchop sandwiches were at Gamers, John's Porkchop shop or at Muzz & Stan's Freeway Bar where they are called Wop Chops. The Freeway also cooks up an awesome fried chicken dinner at the cheapest price in the country – unbeatable!

With many of the immigrants coming to Butte as miners, the pasty was easy to pack into their metal lunchboxes. Oftentimes, my Uncle George would bring home candy in his metal lunchbox on Fridays for all of us kids at a time when 11 of us lived in their very small basement house.

WARNING: Yours may still not turn out to be as good as Joe's or Nancy's, so you might want to stop by sometime in Butte and try one of theirs with gravy preferably.

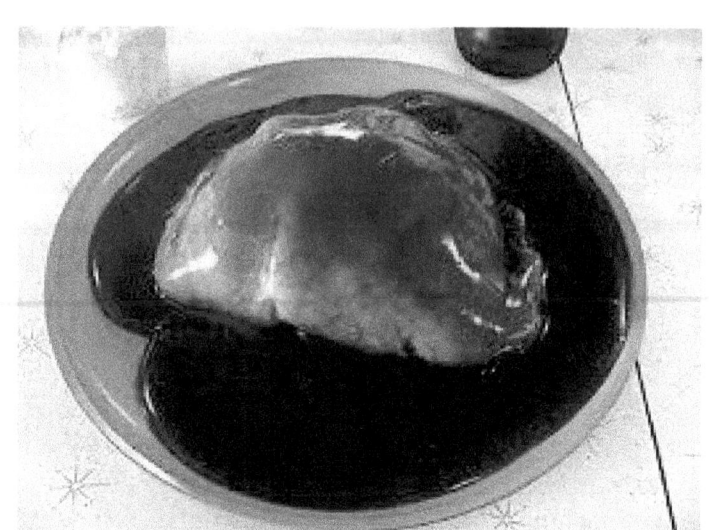

The Butte Pasty – Unequalled and infamous!
Donna Ericson

The pastry:
  3 cups flour
  1 t. salt
  1 1/4 cups vegetable shortening
  1 cup very cold water
The filling:
  3/4# flank steak
  2 or 3 med. potatoes
  1 med. yellow onion
  1 medium turnip
  Salt and pepper
  Butter

Start out by dicing the flank steak, the potatoes and the turnip into small (1/4 to 1/2 inch) cubes. Dice the onion even smaller. Mix the filling ingredients together. Salt and pepper to taste.

Then prepare your pastry dough. Start by mixing the flour and salt together in a bowl. Then cut in the vegetable shortening until it resembles peas. Lastly, pour in the cold water and knead. Divide the dough into six equal parts. Dust your work surface, your rolling pin and your hands thoroughly with flour, then roll each pile of dough into a 6 or 7-inch circle. Fill one half of the circle with filling, leaving 3/4 of an inch empty at the edge. Put a pat of butter (about a teaspoon) on top of the filling. Dab water all round the edge of the circle with a brush to make the edges stick together better. Then fold the empty half over the filled half, and crimp the edges closed with the tines of a fork. Cut a 1" vent in the top of the pasty, and place it on a baking sheet. (Spray the baking sheet with Pam first.) You should wind up with 6 pasties on the sheet.

To make sure the pasties turn a nice golden brown, brush on a mixture of one egg yolk and a T. of water. Then bake in the oven at 400 degrees for 10 minutes, then at 350 degrees for another 40 minutes. To keep the filling moist, dribble a little melted butter mixed with an equal part of water into the vent every 15 minutes. Serve on a plate smothered with a rich, brown gravy. The Montana Cyberzine culinary staff experimented with two packaged gravies 0 Knorr Gravy Classics Hunter Mushroom and Gravy Mix, and French's Mushroom Gravy Mix. They were both extremely easy to make and delicious. Bon appetit!

Teriyaki Honey Chicken
Donna Ericson

1 cut up fryer chicken	1/4 cup dry sherry or water
1/2 cup honey	1 t. grated fresh ginger or 2 t. ground ginger
1/2 cup soy sauce	2 medium garlic cloves, crushed

Place chicken in plastic food storage bag or large glass baking dish. Combine remaining ingredients in small bowl and pour over chicken, turning to coat. Close bag or cover dish with plastic wrap. Marinate in fridge for at least 6 hours, turning two or three times. Remove chicken from marinade; reserve marinade. Arrange on rack over foil-lined broiler pan. Cover chicken with foil. Bake @ 350 degrees for 30 minutes. Uncover; brush with marinade. Bake, uncovered, 30-45 minutes, or until done, brushing occasionally with marinade.

Country Style Oven Ribs
Donna Ericson

The sweet, dark basting sauce on these ribs has a secret ingredient that will keep your family guessing -- it's root beer! For a complete meal, serve the ribs with a side dish of crisp, refreshing coleslaw or fruit salad

Prep: 15 minutes   Bake: 2 hours

1 1/2 t. salt	4 cups root beer (not low calorie)
1/4 t. ground cumin	1/3 cup bottled barbecue sauce
1 t. paprika	2 T. tomato paste
1/2 t. ground black pepper	1 T. vinegar
1/2 t. ground cinnamon	2 t. Dijon-style mustard
1/4 t. ground cloves	1 t. Worcestershire sauce
3 1/2# pork country-style ribs	

1. Preheat oven to 350. In a small bowl combine the salt, cumin, paprika, pepper, cinnamon and cloves. Sprinkle ribs with the spice mixture, rubbing it over entire surface. Place ribs, bone side up, in a shallow roasting pan. Bake, covered, for 1 1/4 hours; drain.

2. Meanwhile, as ribs bake, in a large saucepan bring the root beer to boiling. Boil gently, uncovered, until root beer is reduced to 1 1/4 cups, about 20 to 25 minutes. Remove from heat. Stir in the barbecue sauce, tomato paste, vinegar, mustard and Worcestershire sauce. Return sauce mixture to boiling. Boil gently, uncovered, for 1 minute. Remove from heat; set aside.

3. Turn the drained ribs meaty side up. Spoon about half the root beer sauce over the ribs. Bake, uncovered, for 45 minutes more, basting once or twice with the remaining sauce. Spoon sauce over the ribs to serve. Makes 4 main-dish servings.

Note: After the ribs have baked and you have prepared the sauce, you could finish the recipe in the crock pot.

Lasagna
Lyn Olsen

Brown several pounds of hamburger with salt, pepper, garlic, onion and Italian seasoning. Add several cans of tomato sauce or spaghetti sauce and cook on low covered for 1 hour. Half an hour before you are done cooking, cook 1 pound of lasagna noodles, when done drain. Layer the meat sauce, then noodles, then more sauce, then mozzarella cheese (or ricotta cheese) and layer several times. Cook at 350 degrees until golden brown, about 1 hour.

As a very small child in Montana in the 60's, one of the foods I remember most clearly is my mom's swiss steak. I remember her making this dish on cold dark October nights when the night came early at 5 and leaves had changed their fall colors. I remember the smell of the swiss steak combined with the burning of leaves in our front yards which was a fall tradition in Montana.

Oven Swiss Steak
Myrna Miller

The fork-tender results are sure to remind you of Swiss steak Grandma used to make, with lots of sauce left over for dipping

2 pounds boneless round steak (1/2 inch thick)
1/4 t. pepper
1 medium onion, thinly sliced
1 can (4 oz.) mushroom stems and pieces, drained
1 can (8 oz.) tomato sauce
1 tsp worchestershire
Flour as needed.

Hot cooked noodles

Trim beef; cut into serving-size pieces. Flour and place in fry pan until golden brown on both sides. Then place in a greased 13x9 inch baking dish. Sprinkle with pepper. Top with the onion, mushrooms and tomato sauce. Cover and bake @ 325 degrees for 1 3/4 to 2 hours or until meat is tender. Serve over noodles.

Being raised by my mother with five siblings, four of them boys, there was not much money or food, so my brothers hunting and bringing home deer and elk was a mainstay for us growing up. As a young girl, I wanted to go hunting with my brothers, but it only took one time to convince me otherwise. We left at 4 am on a snowy freezing minus 20 below morning. While I sat in the freezing-cold car out in the middle of nowhere on top of some mountain as the snow continued to fall all day, my brothers went hunting for hours, returning with their deer only after dark had once again fallen.

1905-1910 Gardner Hunting Trip

Hungarian Goulash w/Noodles
Donna Ericson

1# beef cut in cubes
2 medium onions, minced
1/4 t. dry mustard
1 1/4 t. paprika
2 T. brown sugar
1/2 t. salt
3 T. Worcestershire sauce

3/4 t, vinegar
6 T. ketchup
1 1/2 cups water
3 T. flour
Cooked noodles
sour cream and chives (optional)

Brown meat on all sides in Dutch oven. Add onion. Combine mustard, paprika, brown sugar and salt. Combine Worcestershire sauce, vinegar, ketchup. Add to mustard mixture, add to meat. Add 1 c. water; stir, cover. Cook over low heat 2 1/2 hours or till very tender. Blend flour with remaining 1/2 c. water. Add to meat mixture. Stir until thickened. Serve over noodles. Add a dollop of sour cream and a sprinkling of chopped chives, if desired.

Porcupine Meatballs
Donna Ericson

1 pound ground beef
2 cans tomato soup
½ c. uncooked rice
1 egg
½ chopped onion
Salt and pepper

Combine all ingredients except soup. Shape into meatballs and place in baking dish and pour soup over them. Cover and bake at 350 for 1-1/2 hours.

Karen's Hawaiian Meatballs
Donna Ericson (from daughter in law)   excellent

1 1/2# ground beef
2/3 cup cracker crumbs
1/2 cup chopped onions
2/3 cup evap. milk
1 t. seasoned salt
1/3 cup flour
3 T. shortening

Combine all but flour and shortening. Mix lightly, shape meat mixture into balls. Roll in flour. Brown in shortening. Drain excess fat and prepare sauce. Pour sauce over meatballs. Simmer 15 minutes.
Sauce:
1 can (13 1/2oz.) pineapple chunks
2 T. cornstarch
1/2 cup vinegar
1/2 cup brown sugar
1 cup chopped green pepper
2 T. soy sauce
1/2 cup lemon juice
1 T. ch. pimento (opt.)

Drain pineapple and add enough water to juice to make 1 cup. Blend with cornstarch until smooth, gradually, stirring in vinegar, brown sugar, lemon juice and soy sauce. Cook until slightly thickened. Add pineapple, pepper and pimento. Serve over rice or noodles.

Baked Ham with Pineapple
Myrna Miller

Bake ham until almost done. Remove from oven. Cut off skin and score fat side. Insert a whole clove in each square. Set aside. Drain juice from large can sliced pineapple. Put juice, 1-1/2 c. brown sugar, and 1 tsp prepared mustard, dash of ground cloves, 2 tablespoons honey in saucepan and heat to boiling. Remove. Put pineapple rings on ham. Pour sauce over ham and put it back in oven. Cook until well glazed.

Budget Porterhouse Steak
Myrna Miller

1 pound ground beef	½ c milk
1 beaten egg	1 c corn flakes
1-1/2 tsp salt	Chopped onion
Pepper	1 tablespoon worchestershire

Combine ingredients and mix thoroughly. Form into porterhouse steak shape and broil for 5 minutes. Turn and broil on other side then.

Vegetable Lasagna
Donna Ericson

lasagna noodles
3 T. butter or margarine
1 slightly beaten egg
2 T. flour
1 1/2 c. ricotta cheese
1/2 t. dried dill weed
1/8 t. pepper
dash pepper
3/4 pound broccoli, cut up, or
1 c. light cream or milk
1 8-oz. pkg. frozen chopped
1 1/2 c. shredded
  broccoli, thawed
process Swiss cheese (6 oz.)
1/3 c. sliced green onion
1/2 c. grated Parmesan

Cook lasagna noodles in boiling salted water till al dente; immediately drain. Rinse with cold water; drain. Set aside.

Stir together the beaten egg, ricotta cheese, and 1/8 t. pepper. Set aside. If using fresh broccoli cook the broccoli in a small amount of boiling salted water for 5 minutes or till crisp-tender. If using frozen broccoli, cook according to package directions. Drain.

Cook onion in butter till tender but not brown. Stir in flour, dillweed, and dash pepper. Add cream all at once. Cook and stir till bubbly. Cook and stir 1 minute more. Stir in Swiss cheese, stirring till cheese is melted. Stir broccoli into cheese mixture.

Arrange a single layer of lasagna noodles in the bottom of a greased 10x6x2" baking dish. Spread with 1/3 of the ricotta mixture, 1/3 of the cheese-broccoli mixture, and 1/3 of the Parmesan cheese. Repeat the layers of lasagna noodles, ricotta mixture, cheese-broccoli mixture and Parmesan cheese two more times. Cover baking dish with foil. Bake at 350 degrees for 30 minutes. Uncover and bake for 5 to 10 minutes more or till heated through. Let stand 10 minutes before serving. Makes 6 main-dish servings.

Marinades
Donna Ericson

For best results, use your marinade immediately after the ingredients have been combined. Place meats or vegetables in a zip-lock bag with the marinade, and remove as much air as possible before sealing and refrigerating.

You may want to prick the meat with a fork to allow the marinade to permeate deeply into the cut of steak, pork, or chicken.

Shrimp and vegetables may marinate for 15 minutes to 1 hour for best results. All other meats and chicken should be marinated a minimum of 2 hours, and overnight if possible. Marinate meats and then freeze them, so you can use them at a later date with thawing time as your only preparation.

Barbecue Marinade: Combine 1 small finely chopped onion, 1 T. olive oil, 1 T. honey, 3 T. tomato ketchup, 2 T. soy sauce, and 1 t. French mustard in a small bowl and blend.

Basic Steak or Chicken Marinade: Combine 1/2 cup olive oil and 1/2 cup fresh lime juice in a bowl, then add minced garlic, freshly chopped oregano, and crushed peppercorns to taste and pour over chicken or steak.

Brandied Marinade: Combine 1/2 cup brandy, 1/4 cup soy sauce, 2 T. molasses, 1/2 t. Dijon mustard, 1 T. grated fresh ginger, and 1/2 cup dry white wine in a small bowl and mix together until smooth.

Garlic Honey Marinade: Combine 1 small onion (minced), 1/4 cup fresh lemon juice, 1/4 cup sesame oil, 2 T. soy sauce, 2 cloves garlic, (crushed), 1 T. grated fresh ginger, 2 T. honey and 2 t. chopped fresh parsley in a small bowl and mix together.

Honey Mustard Marinade: Combine 1 cup Dijon Mustard, 1 cup dry white wine, 3/4 cup olive oil, 1/4 cup honey, 1 clove garlic (minced) and 2 T. soy sauce in a small mixing bowl.

Lemon Marinade: Mix 2 T. olive oil with 1/2 small onion and 1 clove garlic (both finely minced) in a small bowl. Add 2 T. chopped fresh rosemary, freshly ground black pepper to taste, the zest of one lemon and 1/4 cup fresh lemon juice.

Pork Marinade: Mix 1/2 cup soy sauce with 1/4 cup olive oil and add 2 T. light corn syrup, 2 t. ginger powder, and 1 t. prepared mustard, 1 t. thyme, and garlic and onion powder to taste in a small bowl.

Red Wine Marinade: Combine 2 cups dry red wine with 1 bunch thinly sliced scallions, then mix all together with one clove minced garlic, 1/2 cup olive oil, 1/4 cup soy sauce, 2 T. brown sugar, 1 t. grated fresh ginger and 1 T. Worchestershire sauce. Note: you can use this recipe immediately as a marinade, or you can boil it for ten minutes then use it as a basting sauce.

Spicy Hot Marinade: Mix 4 minced green onions with 2 seeded jalapeno peppers, and add 1/3 cup lemon juice, 1/4 cup honey, 2 T. olive oil, 2 T. fresh thyme leaves (or 2 t. dried thyme leaves). 1/2 t. salt, 1/4 t. ground allspice, and 1/4 t. nutmeg. Blend all until smooth in a blender or food processor.

CHAPTER 4
SIDES
SALADS

Two Apple Salad
Donna Ericson

Can be made up to 1 day ahead.
1/2 cup (2x1/4") julienne-cut fennel bulb (about 1 sm. bulb)
1 1/2 cups (2x1/4") julienne-cut Red Delicious apple
1 1/2 cups (2x1/4") " " Granny Smith apple
1/4 cup finely shredded carrot

1/14 cup sliced green onion
1 T. water
1 T. white wine vinegar
2 t. vegetable oil
1/2 t. sugar
1/4 t. salt

Combine first five ingredients in a medium bowl, toss well. Combine water, vinegar, oil, sugar and salt in a small bowl, stir with a whisk until blended. Add to fennel mixture, toss gently to coat. Cover and chill. 4 servings.

Mom's Frozen Salad
Donna Ericson (Mom Lilian Beaulieu)
Very Good

8 oz. cream cheese
1 green pepper, chopped fine
1 cup drained crushed pineapple
1/2 cup mayonnaise

1/2 cup whipped cream
salt, celery salt, mustard to taste
1/2 cup chopped pecans, if desired

Soften cheese, add rest of ingredients and fold in whipped cream. Freeze. Place squares on lettuce leaves.

Oriental Salad
Donna Ericson

1# pork tenderloin
2 T. brown sugar
1 1/2 T. soy sauce
2 T. sherry wine
1 T. Hoisin sauce
2 T. olive oil
2 T. soy sauce

1 t. grated ginger root
dash tabasco sauce, optional
6 oz. vermicelli
1 cup julienned carrots
1 cup pea pods
4 green onions
1 T. sesame seeds

Cut the pork loin into very thin slices, suitable for stir-frying. Mix the brown sugar, 1 1/2 T. soy sauce, Sherry wine and Hoisin sauce. Pour over the pork strips in a heavy plastic bag. Seal the bag and put the mixture in the refrigerator to marinate for up to one hour, turning the bag occasionally. To prepare the dressing, combine the olive oil, sugar, 2 T. soy sauce, ginger root and Tabasco sauce (or other hot sauce.) Blend and put into the refrigerator to chill. Cook the vermicelli to the desired doneness, adding the pea pods and carrots during the last 2 minutes of cooking. Drain and immediately rinse with cold water. Put into a large bowl. Pour the dressing over the vermicelli mixture, add the green onions, sliced into thin rounds, tops included. Set aside while preparing the pork.

Remove the pork from the refrigerator and put into a hot wok or large skillet. Include some of the marinade. Stir-fry the pork strips until browned and cooked through, about 5-7 minutes. Drain and add to the salad mixture. Mix the salad well. Cover and refrigerate for 1 hour to allow the flavors to blend. If desired, sprinkle with toasted sesame seeds just before serving.

Note: Steamed broccoli flowerets go well in this salad and chopped water chestnuts will add some crunch.

Chicken, Pear and Blue Cheese Salad
Donna Ericson

6 cups torn mixed greens
10-12 oz. grilled or roasted chicken breast, sliced
3/4 cup blue cheese dressing
2 pears, cored and sliced
Fresh ground black pepper

In a large bowl, combine the torn greens, chicken and salad dressing; toss gently to coat. Divide among four large salad bowls or dinner plates. Arrange pear slices on top of salads. Sprinkle with pepper if desired.

Classic Tomato and Mozzarella Salad
Devvi Morgan

4 fresh tomatoes, ripe but not overripe
4 oz. mozzarella
6 fresh basil leaves
1/3 cup olive oil
Salt and freshly ground pepper to taste

Rinse the tomatoes carefully. Remove the tough part where the stem was, then cut tomatoes in half horizontally and remove the seeds. Cut the tomato halves into 1/2 inch squares and place in a serving dish.

Cut the mozzarella into slightly smaller squares and add pieces to the serving dish. Tear the basil leaves into 2 -3 pieces and sprinkle them over the tomatoes and mozzarellas. Season with olive oil and pepper; mix well. Serve cold. Makes 4 servings.

Note: Many restaurants serve this as a composed salad, overlapping alternating rows of tomato slices and mozzarella slices, or scattering mozzarella pieces over a bed of tomato slices and sprinkling the basil over the top.

Summer Shrimp Salad
Donna Ericson

For the dressing:
  1/2 cup vegetable broth
  1 1/2 t. cornstarch
  3 T. fresh lime juice
  2 t. olive oil
  3/4 t. sugar
  1/4 t. cumin
  1/2 T. salt
  1/4 t. pepper

For the salad:
  1# medium shrimp, cooked and peeled
  1 1/2 cups julienne-cut yellow squash
  1 1/2 cups julienne-cut zucchini
  1 1/2 cups cherry tomatoes, 1/2'd
  1 cup fresh corn kernels
  2 T. minced fresh cilantro

Prepare the dressing: Combine broth and cornstarch in a small saucepan, stirring with a whisk; bring to a boil. Cook one minute, stirring constantly. Remove from heat; stir in juice, oil, sugar, cumin, salt and pepper. Cool.

Prepare the salad: Combine shrimp and remaining ingredients in a large bowl. Add dressing mixture to shrimp mixture, tossing well. Makes 4 servings.

How unpredictable and prophetic life can be. One of the most startling memories from my youngest days was when my Aunt Alice took my three brothers to Yellowstone Park, a place we frequented often as a part of growing up in western Montana. It was 1959 on August 16th. Evening had fallen and, not particularly fond of driving at night nor of missing the beauty of the scenery of the park, she had stopped for the night by the Madison River near Hebgen Lake. A more peaceful and scenic sight there could not have been besides the gentle stream of the river, much like the calm before the storm. As the evening wore on, unusual for her, my aunt decided that they should continue on so they left. It was later during that night at 11:37 pm that the mountainside came roaring down at 100 mph when the strongest earthquake to ever hit Montana or the northwest occurred, registering 7.5. Those in the area were killed when the lake spilled over and covered all of the area downstream creating what is now known as Quake Lake. (picture: gendisasters.com)

Spinach Salad Dressing
Donna Ericson

1 cup oil (I use less)
1/4 cup wine vinegar
1 T. Worchestershire

1 t. salt
1 1/3 cup catsup
1 T. minced onion
1/2 cup sugar

Mix and shake all ingredients in jar.

Mandarin Orange Salad
Donna Ericson (from Alice's Herberger Recipe Book)

60 Ritz crackers, crushed
1/4# butter, melted
1/4 cup sugar
6 oz. can unsweetened frozen orange juice, thawed
1 can Eagle Brand condensed milk
8 oz. Cool Whip
2 small cans mandarin oranges, drained

Finely crush crackers. Mix in butter and sugar. Press into 9x13" pan. Reserve a few crumbs for garnish. Blend orange juice with milk. Stir in cool whip and oranges. Fold, do not beat. Pour over crumb crust. Top with reserved crumbs. Refrigerate.

In Montana, at every picnic and barbecue a good macaroni or potato salad was a necessity, and there were many picnics and barbecues whether in our backyards or in the mountains.

Many of our picnics were at my Aunt Donna's house which originally had been a basement home (as seen behind the cousins and brothers in the picture).

I remember when my mom and all six of us kids returned from New Jersey, where we lived for only a couple of years, to live with her family in Butte. In the beginning we lived with my Aunt, her husband and three children in this basement house which had one bathroom, one big room and several bedrooms – for all 11 of us.

Later, an upper floor was added to the house. My Aunt and her daughter, Devvi, delighted in adding Butte charm to the home with the most homey décor and charm, such as painted daisies on the cupboards and brightly multicolored doors for the pantry.

Cauliflower Cashew Salad
Devvi Morgan

"This recipe is great for a big group because it makes a big salad"

Salad:
 1 head iceberg lettuce, washed & torn into small pieces
 1 head cauliflower, washed & cut into bit-side pieces
 2 cups shredded Cheddar cheese
 2 cups seasoned croutons
 2 cups cashews (feel free to add more!)

Dressing: 1 cup mayonnaise or salad dressing
 ½ cup sugar
 ½ cup grated Parmesan cheese

Combine lettuce, cauliflower, cheese, croutons & cashews. Set aside while making the dressing. Stir together the mayonnaise, sugar and Parmesan cheese. The dressing & salad can be made ahead and combined just before serving, making this a great potluck dish. Serves 10-12.

Potato Salad
Lyn Olsen

Boil several pounds of potatoes, can cut up into 4 parts before boiling. Hard boil up to a dozen eggs. Can put a pinprick in the top of the egg to prevent cracking. Can either peel potatoes before or after boiling when cool because skin will come off easier then. Once cool cut potatoes and eggs into squares. Add mayonnaise to moisten in addition to salt and pepper. Add chopped onions if desired as well as mustard and relish if desired.

As American as apple pie and potato or macaroni salad on the 4th of July, soldiers were a major part of every American's life in the first part of the 1900's.

Macaroni Salad
Donna Ericson

2 cups cooked elbow macaroni
1 can (15 oz.) garbanzo beans or chickpeas, rinsed and drained
2 hard cooked eggs, chopped
1/2 cup chopped dill pickles
1/2 cup mayonnaise
1/2 cup applesauce
3 T. chopped onion
3 T. minced fresh parsley
3 T. sliced ripe olives
1 T. mustard seed
1 T. pickle juice
1/2 t. salt
1/4 t. pepper
pinch garlic powder
lettuce leaves
Paprika

In a large bowl combine the 1st 14 ingredients; toss to coat. Cover and refrigerate 1 to 2 hours. Serve in a lettuce lined bowl; sprinkle with paprika. 8 servings

Crab Pasta Salad
Donna Ericson

1 1/2# imitation crabmeat
9 oz. cooked tri-colored pasta
1 can sliced black olives
2 cups dried cranberries
1/2 pkg. frozen petite peas and onions
2 cups toasted pine nuts
Dressing: Balsamic Vinaigrette (1/2 to 3/4 of the bottle)

Layered Pea Salad
Donna Ericson (I made for Duane's Wedding; this is good for a pot luck!)

3 cups torn romaine, salt, pepper, sugar; 6 oz. (1 1/2 cups) shredded Swiss cheese, 4 hard cooked eggs, sliced; 1/2# bacon, crisp cooked, drained and crumbled (10 or 11 slices); 3 cups torn leaf lettuce; 1 (10oz) pkg frozen peas (2 cups) thawed; 3/4 cup mayonnaise; 2 T. sliced green onions with tops.

Place romaine in bottom of large bowl; sprinkle with salt, pepper and sugar. Top with 1 cup of the cheese. Layer eggs atop cheese, standing some slices on edge, if desired. Sprinkle generously with salt. Next, layer in order......the bacon, the leaf lettuce and the peas. Spread mayo over top, sealing to edge of bowl. Cover and chill 24 hours or overnite. Garnish with remaining cheese and green onion. Toss before serving. Serves 10-12. For Duane's wedding, I tripled recipe and used punch bowl.

My cousin Duane (in the very front) was a one-of-a-kind person and so were his many adventures – life was never dull around him. One time he was at our house on Caledonia in Butte and got into his very big black old 56 Chevy and rumbled on down the street. Like in slow motion, we all watched in horror as he collided with the train at the unsignalled tracks a block from our house as Duane stumbled out of the wreck with his glasses dangling to the side.

Pretzel Salad
Donna Ericson

2 C. crushed pretzels (leave some small pieces)
1/4 c. sugar
3/4 c. melted butter or margarine

Combine and spread evenly in 9x13" pan. Bake at 400 degrees for 6 minutes. Cool.

1 8-oz. package cream cheese blended with 1 cup sugar. Add 8-oz. Cool Whip. Spread evenly on cooled pretzel mixture.

1 large box strawberry jello dissolved in 2 cups boiling water. Add 10 oz. packaged frozen strawberries. When nearly set up, spread on cream cheese layer. Let set.

NOTE: you may also use raspberries, or fresh fruit may be used instead of frozen.

Fruit & Nut Tropical Slaw
Devvi Morgan
Serve this first-place slaw with roast ham or pork…

1 8-1/4 ounce can pineapple slices

1 tablespoon lemon juice
1 medium banana (sliced (1 cup)
3 cups finely shredded cabbage
1 cup thinly sliced celery
1 11-ounce can mandarin orange sections, drained
½ cup chopped walnuts (could you substitute macadamia nuts?)
¼ cup raisins
1 8-ounce carton orange yogurt
½ teaspoon salt

Drain pineapple, reserving 2 tablespoons syrup. Cut up pineapple; set aside. Combine the reserved syrup and lemon juice. Coat banana slices with 1 tablespoon of the juice mixture; set aside. In large bowl combine pineapple, banana, cabbage, celery, oranges, nuts and raisins. Blend the reserved juice mixture with the yogurt and salt. Add to cabbage mixture; toss lightly to coat. Cover and chill. Makes 8-10 services.

Almond Chicken Pear Salad
Devvi Morgan

2 cups cooked chicken breast in 1/2 inch cubes
1/2 cup green pepper, diced
1/4 cup diced celery
1/4 t. seasoned salt
1/2 cup plain lo fat yogurt
2 T. mayo
1/2 t. prepared mustard
1/4 t. ground ginger or diced crystalized ginger
2 fresh pears, peeled, cored 1" cubes
lettuce
2 T. toasted sliced almonds

Toss together chicken, green pepper, celery. Sprinkle with seasoned salt. Combine yogurt, mayo, mustard and ginger, add to chicken mixture. Gently mix in pears. Serve on individual lettuce-lined plates. Sprinkle with almonds.

Holiday Waldorf Salad
Donna Ericson

INGREDIENTS:
1 large or 2 sm. pkgs. lemon jello
2 c. boiling water
1 c. cold water
1 T. lemon juice
1/2 c. mayonnaise
1 med. red apple, diced (unpeeled)
1/2 c. diced celery
1/3 c. chopped walnuts, toasted

Dissolve gelatin completely in boiling water in large bowl. Stir in cold water and lemon juice. Refrigerate about 1 1/2 hours or until thickened.

Stir in mayonnaise gradually with wire whisk. Stir in apple, celery and walnuts. Pour into 5-cup mold. Refrigerate 4 hours or until firm.

Confetti Coleslaw
Donna Ericson (Cooking Light) November 2000

Up to one day ahead:
1/4 cup mayo
2 T. cider vinegar
2 T. grated fresh onion
1/2 t. salt
1/4 t. black pepper
2 cups thinly sliced green cabbage
2 cups thinly sliced red cabbage
1/2 cup red bell pepper strips
1/2 cup yellow bell pepper strips
1/2 cup coarsely shredded carrot
1/4 cup raisins

Combine the first 5 ingredients in a medium bowl. Add remaining ingredients, toss gently to coat. Cover and chill. Yield: 5 servings, serving size 1 cup.

Punched-Up Pasta Salad
Start to Finish: 30 minutes

8 oz. Block feta cheese, finely crumbled
¼ cup extra-virgin olive oil
Zest of 1 lemon
1/3 cup thinly sliced sun-dried tomatoes
¼ cup cider vinegar
8 oz. Pasta spirals
2 ears corn

1 small red onion, diced
2 stalks celery finely chopped
2 cups cherry or grape tomatoes, halved
1 green apple, peeled, cored and diced.
2 Tablespoons fresh oregano leaves
Salt and freshly ground black pepper.

In a medium bowl, combine the feta cheese, olive oil, lemon zest, sun-dried tomatoes and vinegar. Toss well and set aside.

Bring a large saucepan of lightly salted water to a boil. Add the pasta and cook according to package directions.

Once the pasta has cooked, drain and rinse under cold water until cool. Let the pasta stand in the colander 5 minutes to drain any excess water. Toss the pasta once or twice during this time.

While the pasta cooks and drains, prepare the corn. To remove the kernels from the corn, start by removing the husk, then stand the ear on the wide end and use a serrated knife to saw down the length of the corn. Discard the cobs.

When the pasta is ready, transfer it to a large bowl. Add the feta cheese mixture and toss well. Add the corn, red onion, celery, tomatoes, apple and oregano. Toss well, then season to taste with sale and pepper.

Makes 6-8 servings.

Devvi's note: I add another apple and blanch (2 minutes) the corn in the cooking water for the pasta. You can also buy the crumbled feta with basil/sun-dried tomatoes. 8/23/08

More on the newspaper article about this recipe:

Start with the pasta, As with many pasta dishes, shape matters. Spirals are best for this sort of salad, as their shape is perfect for trapping the dressing and other ingredients.

It's also important to allow the pasta to drain. The pasta should be dry and a bit tacky or starch when it is combined with the other ingredients; this helps the other flavors to adhere.

For the dressing, oil and vinegar are obvious. Lemon zest adds a wake-you-up freshness and oil-packed sun-dried tomatoes contribute a vital savory, almost mouth-puckeringly good note.

But perhaps most important to the dressing is crumbled feta cheese. Not only does this salty, assertive cheese contribute tons of flavor, its dry texture also serves as sponge for the other flavors in the dressing. This is why the dressing is made first.

Though an unusual addition to a pasta salad, diced green apple provides a fantastic tart flavor that goes so well with the feta cheese. And like the more traditional celery, it also adds a satisfying crunch to contrast the other, softer ingredients.

At this point, you could stop and enjoy this as a typical side salad. To turn it into a meal, several cups of rotisserie chicken meat are all that's needed. Vegetarians could substitute seasoned tofu.

Poppy Seed Dressing
Donna Ericson

1/2 cup sugar	1 t. salt
1/2 cup vegetable Oil	1/4 cup grated onion
1 t. dry mustard	1/2 cup olive oil
1/3 cup wine vinegar	1 ½ t. poppy seeds (opt)

With rotary beater or wire whisk, beat together the sugar, mustard, salt, olive oil, vegetable oil and wine vinegar. Add onion and poppy seeds. Store in tightly closed jar. Will keep in fridge for several weeks.

This dressing is great in a fruit salad and wonderful over bed of mixed greens, topped with slices of pears, crumbled gorgonzola cheese and toasted walnuts (or pecans or pine nuts)

Glorified Rice Salad
Lyn Olsen

My favorite salad! Cook several cups of white rice until done. Let cool. Then add 1 small can of crushed pineapple in its own juice, sweetened red cherries in a jar, a little bit of the red cherry juice from the jar, marshmallows, and whipped cream. Add these a little bit at a time and gently fold until the salad suits your taste.

VEGETABLES/POTATOES

White Sauce
Myrna Miller

One of the most important cooking skills I needed to learn, according to my mom, was to learn how to make a good white sauce because you use these principles in making many other sauces and dishes.

Melt 2 to 3 tablespoons of butter but do not brown or burn. Add 2 to 3 tablespoons flour, couple dashes of salt and let cook over medium until flour is cooked which takes several minutes. Slowly add about ½ c milk, stirring constantly. Do not let thicken too much, keep adding milk so it doesn't get too thick and cook for about another 5 to 10 minutes. Can add anything to the white sauce but we used it with cheese on broccoli and cauliflower for every Thanksgiving dinner and was always our favorite.

Stuffed Baked Potatoes
Myrna Miller

Bake potatoes. Cut in half lengthwise. Scoop out and mash thoroughly. Beat well, adding hot milk until the mixture is soft and fluffy. Season to taste with butter, salt and pepper. Add, if you like, grated cheese, minced green pepper, or ham. Refill the shells. Brush with butter or sprinkle with grated cheese. Set on a baking sheet. Shortly before serving time put ina 450 oven to reheat and brown 8 to 10 minutes.

Potato Cakes
Myrna Miller

Mom always made these as leftovers to use up mashed potatoes.

Shape cold leftover mashed potato in small flat cakes. If the potatoes are too dry to make firm cakes, stir in an egg, slightly beaten. Roll lightly in flour. Brown on both sides in a bacon fat or butter.

Twice Baked Potatoes
Donna Ericson

12 small Yukon Gold potatoes (about 3#)
6 large egg yolks
4 T. butter, softened
1/2 cup heavy cream

1 1/2 cups grated Gruyere cheese
1 T. + 2 t. salt
1/4 t. pepper

Heat oven to 425. Wrap potatoes in aluminum foil, and bake until softened, about 1 hour. Let cool.

When potatoes are cool enough to handle, cut each in half. Scoop out flesh, reserving the skins, and pass through a ricer, or mash by hand. Stir in egg yolks, butter, cream, 1 cup cheese, salt and pepper. Pipe or scoop filling onto reserved skins. Cover with foil and refrigerate until shortly before serving. Heat oven to 400. Place filled potatoes on a baking sheet, and sprinkle with remaining cheese. Bake until filling is set and tops are golden brown, about 25 minutes.

Sunny Sweet Potatoes
Donna Ericson

8 sweet potatoes, about 6 oz. each, peeled and quartered
2/3 cup packed brown sugar
6 T. soft butter
1 T. lemon zest
2 T. fresh lemon juice
2 t. ground ginger
Salt to taste

Simmer the potatoes in boiling water until tender, about 20 minutes. Drain, then mash with the remaining ingredients. Adjust seasonings and serve immediately, or reheat in an ovenproof dish, covered, in a 350 oven.

This is even better with Yams...they have so much more flavor now-a-days!

Roasted Carrots
Donna Ericson

1# carrots
1 small onion, thinly sliced
2 T. butter
1 t. caraway seed
1/2 t. dill seed
1/3 cup water
1 T. honey
1/2 t. salt

Preheat oven to 375 degrees. If you are cooking something else too, like a roast, the carrots are easy; they can cook at pretty much any temperature. Peel the carrots, remove both ends and cut into 2-3" pieces. If the carrots are really thick, cut them in half lengthwise too. (I used the packaged small carrots that are ready to use.) Melt the butter in a saucepan big enough to hold the carrots. Add the onions and cook over med. 3 minutes. Crush the caraway seed and dill seed with a mortar and pestle or the back of a spoon and add to the pan. Cook another two minutes, then add the carrots. Toss to coat, add the water and bring it to a near boil. Pour into a baking dish, drizzle with honey, cover (foil is fine), and place in the oven. Stir every 15-20 minutes. The carrots should be fully cooked but not mushy in about 40 minutes. Try one after half an hour and see how they are doing.

Serves 4 to 6. Prep. time 5 minutes, cooking time nearly 45 minutes.

Old Fashioned Green Beans
Donna Ericson

6 bacon strips, cut into 1/2 inch pieces
2# fresh green beans (or frozen)
3 T. brown sugar
1/2 cup water

In a large skillet, cook the bacon over medium heat until crisp-tender, about 5 minutes. Add the beans, brown sugar and water. Stir gently, bring to a boil. Reduce the heat; cover and simmer for 15 minutes or until the beans are crisp-tender. Remove to a serving bowl with a slotted spoon.

New Potatoes with Herbs and Garlic
Donna Ericson

2 T. olive oil
2 T. ch. fresh sage or 1 t. dried
2 t. ch. garlic
2 t. minced fresh rosemary or
1# sm. red potatoes
1/4 c. or more water
1/4 c. minced fresh parsley

Heat 1 T. oil in heavy medium saucepan over med-hi heat. Add sage, garlic and rosemary; saute until garlic is tender, about 2 minutes. Add potatoes and 1/4 cup water. Reduce heat to med. Cover pan; cook potatoes until just tender, stirring occasionally and adding additional water by T. if potatoes are dry, about 30 minutes. Add parsley and 1 T. oil and toss to coat. Season to taste with salt and pepper. Transfer to bowl and serve.

NOODLES/RICE

Up the hidden, rickety wooden, narrow stairs, we would creep, perhaps like so many before us, to the top. Inside the rooms were dimly lit with secluded seating reminiscent of the former reputation of this Chinese restaurant, Pekin Noodle Parlor in Butte, which once was a whorehouse and opium den. The shadiness and seediness of its history belied the top quality of its food.

(picture Sonny Thornborrow)

Fried Rice
Donna Ericson

3 eggs, lightly beaten
salt and pepper
Pam

Cook eggs in fry pan till set. Cool and roll and slice.

1/4# (3 strips) bacon, cut in 1/4" pieces and fried until crisp. Drain.
4 cups cooked rice, cooled
10oz. frozen peas, thawed

1/3 cup chopped green onions
1/3 cup or less, light soy sauce
2 T. or less oil and a few drops sesame oil

Put oil in fry pan, heat rice, add peas, bacon, eggs, onions and soy sauce.

Herbed Rice Pilaf
Donna Ericson (from Susan Carter- Water Therapy)

1 cup uncooked long grain rice
1 cup chopped celery
3/4 cup chopped onion
1/4 cup butter
2 1/2 cups water
1 pkg. (2-2 1/2 oz.) dry chicken noodle soup

mix
2 T. minced fresh parsley
1/2 t. thyme
1/4 t. rubbed sage
1/4 t. pepper
1 T. chopped pimientos, opt.

In a large skillet, cook the rice, celery and onion in butter, stirring constantly, until rice is browned. Stir in the next six ingredients; bring to a boil. Reduce heat; cover and simmer for 15 minutes. Stir in the pimientos if desired. Remove from the heat and let stand, covered for 10 minutes. 6 servings.

Rodeo Roundup
Donna Ericson

2 T. red wine vinegar
1 T. Dijon mustard
2 t. minced garlic
1/4 cup + 1 t. olive oil
1# small white potatoes, peeled and cut into 1" cubes
Kosher salt
1/4 cup milk

4 10-11" flour tortillas

2 T. butter, softened
2 T. sour cream
2 T. chopped fresh chives
pepper
1 cup corn kernels
1 1/4# London broil, cut into 1/4" strips
1/3 cup bbq sauce

Preheat grill or broiler. Combine the vinegar, mustard, garlic and 1/4 cup olive oil in a large bowl. Add the meat, stir to coat and marinate for 15 minutes.

Place the potatoes and 1 T. kosher salt in a large saucepan and cover with water. Bring to a boil over high heat, reduce heat, and simmer until potatoes are tender when pierced with a fork, about 20 minutes. Drain the potatoes, return to the pan, and mash, using a whisk or a large fork. Add the milk, butter, sour cream, and chives and mix well. Season with 1/2 t. kosher salt and 1/4 t. pepper.

Heat the remaining 1 t. olive oil in a large nonstick skillet over medium heat. Add the corn, 1/2 t. kosher salt and 1/4 t. pepper. Cook until the corn is tender, about 3 minutes. Remove from heat.

Season the beef with salt and pepper. Cook on grill or under broiler until browned but still rare inside, about 5 minutes, turning once. Transfer to skillet with corn. Add bbq sauce and stir to combine.

Divide the potatoes among the tortillas and spread evenly over each tortilla, leaving at least 1" border around the edge. Divide the meat mixture among the tortillas and wrap.

Parmesan Noodles
Donna Ericson

1 pkg. (8 oz.) medium egg noodles
3 T. chopped green onions
garlic salt and pepper to taste

2 T. butter
1/2 cup grated Parmesan cheese

Cook noodles according to package directions; drain. Toss with onions, butter, Parmesan cheese, garlic salt and pepper. Yield: 4 servings.

Potatoes Royal
Devvi Morgan

I got this recipe from the Morgan family, but modified it in the second version below. The men really love this recipe.

"Original Recipe Version"
6 good sized spuds, boiled, peeled and coarsely shredded. Put into buttered 9x13x2 pan.
MIX TOGETHER:
   3 Tbsp. melted butter
   2 cups sour cream
   1 can cream of chicken soup
   1-1/2 cups shredded cheddar cheese.

One more variation:
2 lbs. frozen hash brown potatoes
2 Tbsp. diced onion (or more)
1 pint sour cream
1/2 cup melted butter

salt/pepper
1 can cream of chicken soup
2 cups grated American Cheese

MIX FOR TOP: 1/4 c. melted butter and 2 cups corn flakes. Thaw potatoes well. Mix first 8 ingredients. Place in buttered 9x13 pan. Put butter and corn flake mixture on top. Bake at 350 oven for 45-60 minutes. Pour over spuds and gently mix. Sprinkle ¼ c flake crumbs on top. Bake at 350 for 35 minutes.

Best Macaroni and Cheese
Donna Ericson

Note: Todd and I didn't care for the thyme. I won't use it again. Otherwise, it was delicious!

- 6 T. butter, divided
- 2 T. dry bread crumbs
- 2 T. grated Parmesan cheese
- 1 T. chopped parsley
- 1 1/2 t. chopped fresh thyme or 1/2 t. dried (See note above)
- 1 1/2 t. paprika, divided
- 1/4 cup flour
- 2 t. dry mustard
- 1 t. salt
- fresh grated pepper to taste
- 1/4 t. nutmeg
- 2 1/4 c. milk
- 1/2 cup creme fraiche or sour cream
- 1 clove garlic, peeled
- 8 oz. extra sharp white cheddar, grated divided
- 4 oz. mild cheddar, divided
- 8 oz. elbow macaroni (2 cups raw) cooked, drained and rinsed with cold water and drained well

Preheat oven to 400 degrees, Grease casserole.
In small saucepan melt 2 T. butter. In small bowl combine crumbs, Parmesan, parsley, thyme and 1/2 t. paprika. Toss with melted butter, set aside.

CHAPTER 5

BREAD & BREAKFAST BREADS

Mini Wheat and Nut Muffins
Donna Ericson (quilter friend Eileen Hyslop)

2/3 cup flour
1/4 cup whole wheat flour
1/4 cup chopped almonds or pecans, toasted
1 t. baking powder
1/8 t. soda
1/8 t. salt
1/8 t. nutmeg
1 beaten egg
1/3 cup milk
3 T. packed brown sugar
3 T. cooking oil

Grease eighteen 1 3/4 inch muffin cups or line them with paper bake cups; set aside.

In a large mixing bowl stir together the flour, whole-wheat flour, almonds or pecans, baking powder, soda, salt, and nutmeg. Make a well in the center of the dry mixture, set aside.

In another bowl combine the beaten egg, milk, packed brown sugar and the oil. Add the egg mixture all at once to the dry mixture. Stir just until moistened (batter should be lumpy). Spoon the batter into the prepared muffin cups, filling each two-thirds full. Bake in a 400 degree oven for 10 to 12 minutes or till golden.

Cool in muffin cups on a wire rack for 5 minutes. Remove from muffin cups. Serve warm, or, cool muffins completely. Then place muffins in a freezer bag. Seal, label, and freeze for up to 3 months. Before serving, wrap the frozen muffins in heavy foil and reheat in a 300 degree oven for 12 to 15 minutes or till warm.

Sour Cream Coffee Cake
Gail Vielledent

This is absolutely the best! Moist and delicious!

1 c. butter	1 tsp almond extract
2 c. sugar	2 c. flour
2 eggs	1 tsp baking powder
1 c sour ream	¼ tsp salt

Topping: ½ c. chopped walnuts, 1 tsp cinnamon, ¼ c. brown sugar

Cream butter, sugar, and eggs. Fold in sour cream and almond extract. Sift in dry ingredients and fold carefully. Spoon ½ or 1/3 better into a greased and floured 10" tube or bundt pan (or angel food pan). Cover with ½ topping and add another 1/3 of batter. Add second ½ of topping and last 1/3 of batter. Bake at 350 for 60 minute or until cake begins to pull away at sides and springs back at middle. Cool before removing from pan. Sprinkle top with powdered sugar.

Lemon-sour cream poppy seed muffins
Donna Ericson

High Altitude directions: Heat oven to 350. Stir 3 T. flour into cake mix. Decrease sour cream to 1/2 cup and add 1/2 cup water. Bake about 25 minutes.

1 pkg. pound cake mix
2 t. lemon extract
1 cup sour cream
1 t. vanilla
2 T. poppy seeds
2 eggs
1 T. lemon zest
Lemon glaze (below)

Heat oven to 325. Grease medium muffin cups or line with paper baking cups. Mix all ingredients except glaze in large bowl until well blended. Fill cups 1/2 full. Bake until top springs back when touched lightly or when wooden pick inserted in center comes out clean, about 30 minutes. Cool 10 minutes; remove from pan. Cool completely. Drizzle with Lemon Glaze. About 18 muffins.

Lemon Glaze: Mix 3/4 cup powdered sugar, 1 t. lemon zest and 2 - 3 t. lemon juice in small bowl until smooth. If necessary, stir in additional lemon juice, 1 t. at a time, until desired consistency.

Cinnamon Rolls
Lil Beaulieu

One envelope yeast
4 c flour
1-1/4 tsp salt
¾ c buttermilk
¼ c sugar
6 tablespoons melted butter
3 eggs slightly beaten

Blend buttermilk, butter and eggs. Mix the flour with sugar, yeast and salt and then add to liquids. Stir until batter sticks together. Put on floured board and knead to form round nonsticky ball about 10 minutes. Place in oiled bowl and cover, let rise in warm area until doubled, about 2 hours. Roll out on floured board into large rectangle until about ½ inch thick. Brush with melted butter. Shake cinnamon/sugar mixture over all of the dough except for edges. Roll up and cut into 1 inch sections, place in greased cake pan and cover. Let rise until doubled in warm area. Can either cover with powdered sugar glaze or sticky caramel nut topping (1/2 c brown, ½ c. light corn syrup, 4 tablespoons butter melted, dash of salt, ½ tsp vanilla and several cups of chopped nuts (pecans or walnuts or almonds).

Sourdough Bread
Lyn Olsen

1 pkg yeast   ¾ c. milk
¼ c. warm water   1 c flour

Add yeast to warm water. Mix remaining ingredients in. Cover and let sit for several hours til starting to fermenting. Then add to 1 c of above mixture, 2-1/2 c flour and 2 c warm water. Cover with lid and let rise for 24 to 48 hours til well fermented. After fermenting, add 4 c flour, 1 tsp salt, 3 tablespoons sugar, ¼ tsp soda, and 3 tablespoon oil. Mix and knead and prepare as desired; let rise until doubled and bake at 350.

Swedish Bread
Myrna Miller

Put in a mixing bowl: 1 cup lukewarm milk and 1 package yeast. Let stand for 5 fimnutes. Stir. Add ½ cups soft butter, 1/3 cup sugar, 1 egg beaten, ¼ teaspoon salt, ½ teaspoon almond extract. Mix thoroughly. Add enough flour to knew the dough well. Let rise until about double in size. Shape in a braid or ring. Let rise. Bake about 20 minutes at 350.

Oatmeal Bread
Lyn Olsen

6 c flour	1 c oatmeal
2-1/2 tsp salt	2 c. boiling water
2 tablespoons butter	2 pkg yeast
½ c honey	1/3 c warm water

Pour boiling water over oats in a large bowl. Add salt, butter, honey. Soak yeast in warm water. Stir yeast and when dissolved add to slightly cooled oats mixture. Stir in 2 c flour and mix, then 2 c of flour again, stir and the last 2 c flour. Knead until smooth and elastic. Place dough in well greased bowl. Cover with cloth and let rise until doubled. Knead down and divide and place in 2 well greased bread pans. Cover and let rise again until double in size. Bake at 325 for 50 minutes.

Banana Bread
Donna Ericson

Bake in 9x5x3 loaf pan. Can be doubled & baked in 2 large & 1 small loaf pans. Triple recipe & make 3 large & 2 medium loaves.

1 cup sugar
1/2 cup margarine
2 eggs
1-1/2 cup mashed bananas
1 T. lemon juice
2 cup flour
3 tsp baking powder
1/2 tsp salt
1 cup chopped nuts.

Cream sugar & margarine. Add eggs, one at a time, beating well after each. Stir in bananas & lemon juice. Sift flour with baking powder and salt, add & mix quickly. Stir in nuts. Bake at 350 degrees one hour or until done when tested. Cool on rack.

Banana Bread
Lyn Olsen

One of the best banana bread recipes ever!

½ c. butter
2 eggs
1 c. sugar
Pinch of salt

2-3 bananas mashed
2 c. flour
½ c. nuts if desired

Cream butter and sugar, add eggs, flour and salt, bananas and nuts. Pour into greased loaf pan and bake at 350 degrees for 45 minutes.

Bacon and Gruyere Muffins
Donna Ericson

7 or 8 thin slices bacon
2 cups flour
2 T. sugar
1 T. bak. powder
1/2 t. salt
1 large egg

4 T. unsalted, melted butter
1 cup milk
2 T. sour cream or plain yogurt
3/4 cup finely diced Gruyere or Swiss cheese

Preheat oven to 400 degrees. Grease 9 standard muffin cups with butter or butter-flavored nonstick cooking spray; fill the unused cups one-third full with water to prevent warping.

In a fry pan over medium-hi heat, cook the bacon slices until crisp, 6-8 minutes, turning as needed. Using tongs, transfer to paper towels to drain. Let the bacon cool, then crumble. Set aside.

In a bowl, stir together flour, sugar, baking powder and salt.

In another bowl, whisk together the egg, melted butter (see note), milk and sour cream or yogurt to the dry ingredients and stir just until evenly moistened. The batter will be slightly lumpy.

Using a large rubber spatula, fold in bacon and cheese just until evenly distributed, no more than a few strokes. Do not over mix.

Spoon the batter into each muffin cup, filling it level with the rim of the cup.
Bake until golden, dry and springy to the touch, 20 to 25 minutes. A toothpick inserted into the center of a muffin should come out clean. Transfer the pan to a wire rack and let cook for 5 minutes. Unmold the muffins. Serve warm or at room temperature. Note: For added bacon flavor, replace 2 T. of melted butter with 2 T. bacon fat. If not serving the muffins immediately, store in the refrigerator. These muffins are great accompaniments to soups, salads and omelets. Makes 9 muffins.

Cheerios
Lyn Olsen
A staple of ours for many years as children....
Melt several tablespoons of butter and then add 1 to 2 cups of cheerios, stirring while they cook. Take off heat and add a couple of tablespoons of sugar so the cheerios become coated.

Blueberry Muffins
Donna Ericson

6 T. unsalted butter, softened, plus more for tins
3 cups plus 2 T. flour
3 t. baking powder
1 t. salt
1 3/4 cups sugar, plus more for sprinkling
1 large whole egg, plus 2 large egg yolks
1 t. vanilla
1 cup milk
1 3/4 cups wild or cultivated blueberries

1. Butter large (3 3/4 inches) or small (2 3/4 inches) muffin tins; set aside. Preheat oven to 375 degrees. In a bowl, sift flour, baking powder and salt; set aside.

2. In the bowl of electric mixer cream butter and sugar on med. speed until fluffy, about 3 minutes. Add eggs and vanilla; mix until well combined. Reduce speed to low; alternate adding reserved flour mixture and milk to mixer, beginning and ending with flour. Remove bowl from mixer; gently fold in berries by hand.

Divide batter among muffin tins; sprinkle generously with sugar. Bake until light golden, about 45 minutes for large, about 30 minutes for small. Cool in pan 15 minutes. Remove from pan; transfer to cooling rack.

Red Velvet Pancakes
Lyn Olsen

1 1/2 cups all-purpose flour
2 tablespoons unsweetened cocoa powder
2 tablespoons white sugar
1/3 cup powdered sugar
1 1/2 teaspoons baking powder
1 teaspoon ground cinnamon
1 teaspoon salt
1 cup milk
¾ c butter melted
2 large eggs
1 teaspoon vanilla extract
2 tablespoons white vinegar
1 tablespoon red food coloring

Mix all of the dry ingredients together in a bowl. Mix the remaining ingredients together in another bowl, and then add to dry ingredients. Warm pan at medium high, and cook as a regular pancake with pan lightly greased and batter slightly thin…add more milk if the mixture needs to be runnier to make good pancakes. Brown on one side and then turn to brown on the other side.

Macadamia Nut French Toast
Devvi Morgan

6 large eggs
1/4 cup sugar
1/2 t. nutmeg
1 cup orange juice
1/2 cup whole milk
1 t. vanilla
1 16-oz loaf French bread, sliced into 1-inch thick pieces
2/3 cup butter
1/2 cup chopped macadamia nuts

Mix eggs, sugar, nutmeg, juice, milk and vanilla in large bowl. Place bread slices in a single layer in 13x9-inch baking pan. Pour egg mixture over bread, turning each slice to make sure each slice is well covered. Cover and refrigerate overnight. In the morning, heat oven to 400 degrees and melt butter in a 15x10inch jelly roll pan. Place egg-saturated bread slices in pan and bake for 10 minutes. Turn slices, sprinkle nuts on top and bake for an additional 10 minutes, or until nicely browned. Sift powdered sugar over top before serving. Yields 13-15 pieces, depending on loaf size.

Sweet Waffles
Lyn Olsen

Undoubtedly the best waffles ever.

½ c. butter
2/3 c. milk
¾ c. sugar
1 c. flour
3 eggs

Cream together butter and sugar. Combine eggs and milk. Add egg mixture alternately with flour to creamed mixture. Beat til smooth and drop onto waffle maker and bake until brown.

Royette Maki's Povitica (or is it Potica)

(Po va teet' sa)
Donna Ericson
This is a very traditional Butte/Anaconda (Yugoslavian nut bread, many times used as a grooms cake at a wedding and served during the holidays and other special occasions).

Filling - can be made day ahead, refrigerated and brought to room temp. when ready to use:

1 1/4# walnuts, ground with 1 cup raisins
3 cups honey (Blue Star if possible)
1 cup milk

Bring to boil, add 1 T. butter and 1 T. vanilla

Boil slowly 1/2 hour. Remove from heat, let set 5 minutes then 1 at a time add 3 eggs, mix each one like hell so it doesn't cook before it mixes. Cool.

Melt 1# butter. Use 1/2 cup to make dough and use what is needed of what's left to spread on dough before adding filling.

Dough: 2 pkgs. yeast, 2 T. warm water 1 t. sugar. Let set till bubbly. Beat with fork 3 eggs, add 1/2 cup sugar, 1/2 cup melted butter, 1 cup warm water, 1 t. salt. Add yeast mixture. Sift in gradually 5 or 6 cups flour. Let rise double once.

Pin sheet or table cloth as tightly as you can on table so surface is smooth. Flour cloth heavily to prevent dough from sticking. Roll out and pull out dough until very thin. Spread melted butter over entire area. Spread filling over entire area. Turn over 1" of dough around entire povitica, then roll onto piece of aluminum foil. Shape as desired. Lift into roaster or desired pan. Let rise 45 minutes to 1 hour, covered with dish towel. Put into preheated 350 degree oven for 1 hour, sometimes 10 - 20 minutes longer.

When you remove it from oven, rub top of poviticia with butter to prevent crust from becoming hard. Let cool completely.

Pumpkin Loaves
Donna Ericson

Grease 4 small pans. Add wax paper on bottom and grease that. Preheat oven to 325 degrees.

2 cups + 2 T. flour
1 t. nutmeg
1/2 t. salt
2 cups less 2 T. sugar
1/2 t. baking powder
3/4 cup butter or margarine
1 t. soda
2 eggs
1 t. cloves
1 16 oz. can
1 t. cinnamon
pumpkin (2 cups)

Sift dry ingredients into large bowl. At med. speed beat sugar with butter just until blended. Add eggs, 1 at a time. Beat well after each. Continue to beat till light and fluffy. Beat in pumpkin. At low beat in flour mixture till combined. Turn evenly into 4 pans. Bake 1 hour or till toothpick checks clean. Cool in pans 10 minutes. Turn onto wire racks to cool completely.

Edna's Biscuits
Donna Ericson (Edna Cass was Donna's aunt from Toston, Montana - a good and easy ranch recipe)

Preheat oven to 450 degrees
Sift together 3 times:
   2 cups flour
   2 t. baking powder, slightly rounded
   1 t. salt
Cut in 1/2 cup Crisco. Add 1/2 to 2/3 cup milk (to make soft dough)
Knead gently on lightly floured board 10 times.
Cut and bake 15 minutes or till brown.

Eggs A La Suisse
Myrna Miller

Melt in a small omelet pan, 1 tablespoon butter. Add ½ cup cream and add 4 eggs, one at a time with beating after each egg. Sprinkle with salt and pepper. Cook slowly until whites are nearly firm, then sprinkle with 2 tablespoons cheese. Continue cooking until firm.

Date Nut Bread
Donna Ericson

3 large loaves
or
1 large and 5 small

1# dates, cut up (12/22/01 I used Sunsweet chopped dates in
    round cardboard box. I used all of 1 - 10 oz. and most of
    another.)
3 t. soda
3 cups boiling water
3 T. butter
Cut up dates. Add boiling water, soda and butter and set aside to cool. (12/22/01 I didn't cut up the dates. Used them just as they came from the box).

Blend 3 cups sugar -3T. and 3 eggs. Add date mixture and blend well. Add 4 1/2 cups sifted flour +3T., 1 1/2 t. salt and 2 cups chopped walnuts and stir just to blend. Pour into 3 greased loaf pans and bake 1 hour @ 350 degrees (325 for glass pans). (I used 1 large pan and 5 small ones.)

Bananas Foster Waffles
Donna Ericson

6 T. (3/4 stick) butter
3/4 cup maple syrup
3/4 t. cinnamon
1/4 cup dark rum (optional) I used it
1 t. vanilla

4 bananas, peeled and cut diagonally into
1/2" thick slices
4 large waffles
Sweetened whipped cream for serving I used
cool whip

In large saute pan over med. heat, melt butter with maple syrup. Stir in cinnamon, rum and vanilla; simmer 1 minute.

Add bananas to pan; cook 2 - 3 minutes. Using slotted spoon, transfer bananas to serving plate. Pour maple syrup mixture into saucebboat. Serve immediately with waffles and whipped cream. I just put the banana mixture on top of the waffles and added the cool whip. Enjoy

SCRAMBLED EGGS
Lyn Olsen

Crack as many eggs as you want into a pan which has been coated with butter. Stir the eggs as they cook so they are scrambled. Add salt and pepper to taste. Add sour cream and cheese a few minutes before eggs are done and mix together.

Crepes

Lyn Olsen

Crepes can be filled with absolutely anything. When I went on an exchange program in Paris during college I would eat crepes on every corner with sugar on them.

3 eggs slight beaten	1 c. milk
6 tablespoons flour	Butter
¼ tsp salt	

Beat eggs, flour and salt until smooth. Add milk and beat until smooth. Cover and chill ½ to 1 hour if possible. Stir batter well before using. When ready, heat some butter at the bottom of a fry pan big enough to make a round crepe, and then pour about a half cup of batter onto the pan, tilting pan to spread the dough around the pan and create a thin layer but make sure heat is hot, but not too hot and cook until brown, then flip and brown on the other side.

Benson's Savory Eggs
Devvi Morgan (Benson is hiking friend from the Missoula Mountaineers)

8" sq. pan. For 9x13" double recipe.

1 c. cheddar cheese (grate and put into buttered pan)

Combine:
- 1/2 cup cream
- 1 t. prepared mustard
- 1/2 t. salt
- 1/4 t. pepper
- 6 eggs, slightly beaten
- any herbs desired, such as oregano, thyme, nutmeg

Gently pour over cheese.

Bake @ 325 degrees for 25 minutes or until set and lightly browned on top.

SANDWICHES

Growing up in Butte in the 70's was a time when we kids could stay out and go anywhere without fear, so sleepouts were common. During the sleepouts, as 12 and 13-year-old girls we could run through the neighborhood in the late night hours (after the streetlights went on) around 11 or 12. Later, we would fix our sleeping bags on our porches or yards with no concerns of danger. During those sleepouts our ritual was making tuna cheese bake sandwiches.

Tuna Cheese Bake Sandwiches
Lyn Olsen

Mix tuna fish with mayonnaise or miracle whip and put on a piece of bread. Top with American cheese and toast in the oven until golden brown.

Chicken BLT
Donna Ericson

2/3 cup mayonnaise
1 - 2 T. prepared horseradish
4 boneless, skinless chicken breast halves
4 sandwich buns, split
lettuce leaves and tomato slices
8 slices crisp cooked bacon

Combine mayo and horseradish; reserve 1/3 cup. Brush chicken with remaining mayo mixture; grill or broil 7 to 10 minutes, just until cooked through.
Spread rolls with reserved mayo. Top with lettuce, tomato, bacon and chicken.

Greek Chicken Sandwiches
Donna Ericson

Sauce:
   1 cup (8 oz.) plain lowfat yogurt
   2 T. each fresh lemon juice and chopped dill
   1/2 t. minced garlic

2 cups shredded cooked chicken
2 T. fresh lemon juice
1/2 t. salt
4 pocketless pitas, warmed, or flour tortillas

Toppings:
   1/2 cup thinly sliced onion
   2 plum tomatoes (such as Roma), sliced
   2 cups shredded lettuce

Mix all of the Sauce ingredients in a medium bowl.

Combine chicken, lemon juice and salt in another bowl. Spoon on pitas, add Toppings, then spoon on sauce. Roll up; eat out of hand.

Turkey Club Wrap w/Avocado Cream
Donna Ericson

Can be doubled
2 servings
1 12" whole wheat tortilla
2 T. avocado cream (recipe follows)

1/4# sliced roast turkey
5 slices crisp cooked bacon
5 thin slices tomatoes
3 leaves red leaf lettuce

Place tortilla on a work surface and spread with avocado cream. Layer turkey, tomato and lettuce over the tortilla, leaving a border of at least 1" all around edge; roll tightly, wrap in plastic wrap or foil and then in wax paper and chill until ready to serve. Cut diagonally in 1/2 and serve.

Avocado Cream:
   1 ripe avocado, peeled and pitted
   2 or 3 T. sour cream
   1 1/2 T. chopped fresh cilantro
   1 T. fresh lime juice
   1/4 t. salt
   1/8 t. ground cumin
   1 clove garlic, 1/4'd

Add all ingredients to food processor or blender and pulse to make a rough puree. Refrigerate until ready to use. Store in airtight container for up to 3 days.

Sloppy Joe
Donna Ericson

3/4 cup chili sauce
3 T. tomato paste
1 T. Worchestershire
1 T. red wine vinegar
2 t. dried oregano
1 t. ground cumin
2 T. olive oil
1 cup diced yellow onion
Kosher salt
pepper

3/4# lean ground beef
1/2# spicy sausage, removed from the casing and crumbled
2 cups cooked long grain white rice, warm
1/2 cup thinly sliced green onion, green part only
1/2 cup sour cream
4 10-11" flour tortillas, flavored suggestion, salsa or tomato

Combine the chili sauce, tomato paste, Worchestershire sauce, and vinegar in a small bowl. Stir in the oregano and cumin and set aside.

Heat the olive oil in a large nonstick skillet over medium heat and add the ground beef and sausage. Season with the remaining 1/2 t. kosher salt. Cook until the meat is completely browned, 6-8 minutes. Add the onion mixture, rice, and green onion and mix well.

Divide the sour cream among the tortillas and spread evenly over each tortilla, leaving at least a 1" border around the edge. Divide the meat mixture among the tortillas and wrap.

A Simpler Version of Sloppy Joe
Myrna Miller

2 pounds ground beef
1 large onion
3 tablespoons brown sugar
2 tsp worchestshire sacue
1 tablespoon dry mustard

¼ c ketchup
1 can tomato sauce
Salt and pepper
Dash of chili powder

Fry beef and add all ingredients. Simmer for 2 hours.

Homebaked Macaroni and Cheese
Myrna Miller

Cook one package of macaroni until slight tender, do not use quick cook macaroni. Make white sauce: Melt 4 tablespoons of butter, do not brown. Add enough flour (approximately 6 tablespoons) until butter and flour form a smooth runny mixture, not too thick. Cook on medium stirring constantly. Cook for several minutes so that the flour cooks. Add ½ cup of milk and continue to cook, stirring constantly. Continue adding milk and do not let mixture become too thick or lumpy, but let it thicken some. Continue adding milk until mixture is semi-thick after cooking for awhile. Add salt and pepper. Add as much cheese (any kind) to white sauce mixture, approximately 2 cups. Pour over macaroni in baking dish and top with cheese. Bake at 350 degrees for 1 hour.

CHAPTER 6
DESSERTS

PIES

Never Fail Pie Crust
Donna Ericson (Dorothy Reed long time friend)

2 cups Crisco shortening
4 1/2 cups flour
1 t. baking powder
1 t. salt
1 egg
1 T. vinegar

Put egg and vinegar in 1 cup measure. Beat, then fill with cold water.

Blend Crisco shortening, flour, baking powder and salt till like coarse meal. Add water mixture and stir until incorporated. Make into patty sized rolls, put into individual sandwich bags and freeze until ready to use. Makes about enough for 2 double and 1 single pies.

Cinnamon Pie Crust
Myrna Miller

Take leftover pie crust, roll it out, the shape doesn't matter at all, place it on a cookie sheet, and spread butter on it like spreading butter on toast, then sprinkle a mixture of sugar and cinnamon over it. Bake at 350 degrees until golden brown.

This can also be done with flour tortillas. Place the tortillas in a fry pan with just enough hot grease that the tortilla floats on it; do not have the temperature too high, about medium high heat. Brown one side, then the other, then remove and spread the butter on it, and sprinkle the cinnamon/sugar mixture as desired.

Shredded Apple Custard Pie
Donna Ericson

Pastry for 9" single crust pie
4 eggs
3/4 cup sugar
1/4 cup melted butter
1 t. vanilla
1/2 t. grated lemon peel
1/4 t. each ground cinnamon and nutmeg
about 3 large tart pales
sweetened whipped cream (opt)

Prepare pastry, using a mix or a favorite recipe. Roll out dough and fit into a 9-inch pie pan; flute edge.

Lightly beat the eggs; add the sugar and beat until well blended. Stir in the butter, vanilla, lemon peel, cinnamon and nutmeg.

Peel the apples and coarsely shred, using a food processor or shredder with large holes; you need 3 cups shredded apples (pack lightly to measure). Stir apples into egg mixture; turn this filling into pastry shell.

Bake pie on the lowest rack of a 425 degree oven for 10 minutes. Reduce temperature to 350 degrees and bake 35 to 40 minutes longer, or until a knife inserted in center comes out clean. Let cool on a wire rack. Serve warm or chilled; top with dollops of whipped cream if desired. 6 servings.

Pecan Pie
Lyn Olsen

¾ c. brown sugar
4 eggs beaten
1 tsp vanilla
Pinch salt
1 tablespoon melted butter
1 c. white karo syrup
1-1/2 c. pecans (the more the better)

Beat eggs, add karo syrup and rest of ingredients. Preheat oven to 350 and when ready place pie in oven for 45 to 50 minutes.

Lemon Meringue Pie
Lyn Olsen

Made this pie a million times and it is everyone's ultimate favorite. This recipe is the only one I found that makes a really good pie.

Prepare regular pie shell and bake.

½ teaspoon salt
2-1/4 c. boiling water
3 egg yolks (separate and keep whites for meringue)
¾ c. sugar
7 tablespoons flour
2 tablespoon cornstarch (make sure it is good)
½ c. sugar
6 tablespoon lemon juice
3 tablespoon grated lemon rind

On medium heat, combine ¾ c. sugar with flour, cornstarch, and salt. Slowly stir in boiling water and cook stirring constantly, until smooth and just thick enough to mound. If you want the pie to be thicker cook just a little longer. Beat egg yolks with ¼ c. sugar and then slowly stir into hot mixture, stirring constantly. Cook 5 minutes. Add lemon juice and rind and remove from heat. You can add more lemon juice and rind to get consistency of flavor that you want, so if you want it more tart, then add more lemon juice. Pour in baked pie shell. Top with meringue which is made as follows; Make sure egg whites are at room temperature. You have them leftover from pie recipe. You can add a couple more egg whites if you like lots of meringue. Beat egg whites in bowl deep enough at high speed for mixer. Add ¼ teaspoon salt and ½ teaspoon vanilla. Beat until frothy. Start adding sugar one tablespoon at a time up to 6 tablespoons (more if you used more egg whites) and keep beating after each sugar is added. Beat until stiff, then drop by spoonful onto pie and swirl up so that it forms peaks on the pie and make sure it covers to the edges. Bake 12 to 15 minutes at 350 until golden brown. Do not put this pie in a closed container as it has a lot of moisture and the moisture will deflate and make everything runny.

Mom's Strawberry/Rhubarb Pie
Donna Ericson (Lilian Beaulieu)

2 cups rhubarb
2 cups strawberries

Mix 1 1/2 cups sugar, 5 T. flour, 1/8 t. salt, 2 eggs till frothy. Put 1/2 of the fruit in pastry lined pan, add 1/2 of sugar mixture, add rest of fruit, rest of sugar mixture and dot with butter. Add top crust, bake at 425 degrees for 35 minutes or till brown.

Deep Dish Apple Pie
Donna Ericson

Apples	1/4 cup flour, mixed with sugar
orange and lemon zest	1 t. salt
1 T. orange juice	3/4 t. cinnamon
1 t. lemon juice	1/2 t. nutmeg
1/2 cup sugar or more if apples are very tart	1/8 t. allspice

Mix all the ingredients in large bowl. Place above ingredients in processor pie dough. Place top crust over pie. Brush with egg wash made with 1 egg and 1 T. milk or water Sprinkle with small amount of sugar. Bake @ 400 degrees 1 hour or 1 hour and 15 minutes till golden brown.

CAKES & FROSTINGS

Growing up, all the kids hung out together all day and night until the street lights came on and parents began the onerous task of calling their kids repeatedly to stop playing and come in. Everyone watched out for everyone else in the neighborhood back then.

One of my friend's grandmother was a superb baker and decorator of the most beautiful made-from-scratch cakes for this was a time that people did not buy cakes from the grocery stores nor did they use mixes or canned frostings. One time for a birthday, the grandmother had baked and decorated the most beautiful cake ever and asked my friend who was about 10 at the time to carry the cake to her parents' house for the birthday party; however, before her lay a high dirt hill upon which sat train tracks. Struggling her best to balance the cake and grabbing at the weeds in the dirt clumps on the hillside to steady her feet, she could feel her feet slipping beneath her, and like Jack and Jill, she and the cake came tumbling down the hill.

Lemon Coconut Filling
Donna Ericson

1 1/2 cups powdered sugar	1 t. grated lemon peel
2 egg yolks	1/8 t. salt
1 1/2 t. cornstarch	1 cup flaked coconut

Mix sugar, cornstarch and salt in small saucepan. Add lemon juice and egg yolks, blend well. Cook over low heat, stirring constantly, until slightly thickened, about 10 minutes. Remove from heat and stir in lemon peel and coconut. Cool. Spread between cake layers or use as cake topping.

Scrumptious Cake topping
for filling and top of 8-9 inch layers or top of 9x13
Donna Ericson

1 cup walnuts	1 cup table cream
4 egg yolks	few grains salt
1 cup sugar	1 t. vanilla

Grind walnuts or chop very fine. Beat egg yolks lightly and combine with sugar, cream and salt. Place over boiling water and cook and stir until thick. Remove from heat and blend in vanilla. Cool. Stir in walnuts and spread on cooled cake.

Coconut Pecan Frosting Or German Chocolate Frosting
Myrna Miller – the very best frosting ever!

Absolutely the best frosting ever – beats canned anytime! I only made this for very special people because it takes time and it is one of the best things you can ever eat!

Melt 1/4 c. butter in 1 c. evaporated milk, 1 cup sugar with 3 beaten egg yolks over medium heat on the stove for about 10 minutes. Add vanilla, 1 cup coconut and 1 cup chopped nuts, can add more nuts and coconut if desired.

Fluffy White Frosting
Myrna Miller

1/2 cup cold water	1/4 t. salt
1 3/4 cups sugar	1/4 t. cream of tartar
2 egg whites	1 1/2 t. vanilla

Place water, egg whites, cream of tartar, sugar and salt in upper part of double boiler. Beat with rotary egg beater until thoroughly mixed. Place over rapidly boiling water, beat constantly with egg beater and cook about seven minutes or until frosting will stand in peaks. Remove from heat, add vanilla. Stir until thick enough to pile well

Red Velvet Frosting
Donna Ericson (from card friend Ione McCarthy)

3 T. flour
1 cup milk

Mix and cook until thick and smooth, stirring constantly. Set aside to cool.

Cream 1 cup granulated sugar with 1 cup butter and 1 t. vanilla. Mix well with mixer. Add flour and milk mixture, 1 t. at a time, beating until fluffy.

No such thing as canned frosting in those days, so every cake was topped with homemade frostings - absolutely delicious! I remember thinking canned frosting and boxed cake mixes would be a flop because nobody would prefer those over a real home-baked cake! When I was in 5th grade, I remember my mom teaching me how to make a cake – I failed miserably many times. Between this and teaching me bowling, my mom one day in exasperation told me she gave up and I was never going to learn either. Since, I have baked more cakes for which I have become famous as well as bowling with scores in the high 200's. The bowling was perfected amongst all of us Olsen kids by bowling every Saturday at Star Lanes in the kids leagues where we earned many a badge and trophy.

Caramel Fudge Icing
Myrna Miller

2 c. brown sugar
1 c sugar
1 c sour cream or sour milk

1 tablespoon butter
1 tsp vanilla

Combine sugars and sour cream. Cook stirring constantly until a small amount forms a soft ball when dropped into cold water. Add butter and vanilla and cool to lukewarm without stirring. Beat until thick enough to spread. If frosting becomes too thick while spreading, beat in a few drops of hot water.

Extra Special Whipped Cream Frosting
Lyn Olsen

2 c. solid vegetable shortening (can substitute 1 c butter or margarine and 1 c solid vegetable shortening).
2 pounds confectioner's sugar (4 cups to a pound)
½ tsp salt
1 to 2 tsp clear vanilla or flavoring
6 to 8 oz whipping cream

Cream shortening until fluffy. Add sugar and continue creaming until well blended. Add salt, flavoring and whipping cream. Blend on low speed until moistened. Beat at high speed until icing is fluffy.

Penuche Frosting
Myrna Miller

As kids, many of our cakes were covered with this excellent frosting.

½ c butter
1 c. brown sugar
¼ c cream
1-3/4 to 2 c powdered sugar

Melt butter in saucepan. Add brown sugar. Boil over low heat for 2 minutes, stirring constantly. Stir in cream. Bring to boil stirring constantly. Cool. Gradually add powdered sugar, beating until smooth. If icing becomes too thick, add a little boiling water.

Never fail 7 min. icing
Myrna Miller
1-1/2 cup sugar, 2 egg whites, 1/4 t. cream of tartar, 1-1/2 tsp white Karo, 1/4 t. salt, 1/3 c cold water.

Put all ingredients into double boiler, cook and beat with mixer until spreading consistency and forming peaks, about 7 minutes. Add 1 t. vanilla. (Same amount of brown sugar and dark Karo may be used.)

Easy Caramel Frosting
Donna Ericson

1 cup brown sugar	1/3 cup cream or canned milk
1/2 cup white sugar	2 T. butter
dash salt	1 T. Karo

Mix, bring to boil, stirring constantly. Boil 1 minute. Cool to lukewarm. Add 1/2 t. vanilla and beat till thick.

Auntie Alice owned, I believe, the first convertible Volkswagen in Butte. In fact, for this reason, she was chosen to drive Santa Claus at Christmas time through the uptown area of Butte. These were very carefree times when us kids would sit on the convertible top when it was down. She taught all of us kids to drive in this car, brave soul, and she drove it until the floor boards rusted through. When we lived on Caledonia Street, our house had a front porch which was about 15 steps up, so we kids would all pick up her VW and put it on the porch to mystify her as to how her car got there. My first car was also an VW bug and I couldn't kill that anything – it always would run - even when the starter went out – I would park on the hills in Butte so I could roll it down and then it would start.

Dream Frostings
Donna Ericson

Quick fluffy lemon frosting:
- 1 1/2 cups cold milk
- 1 envelope Dream Whip
- 1 sm. lemon instant pudding and pie filling

Pour milk into a deep narrow-bottom mixer bowl; add DreamWhip and pudding mix. Beat at lo speed of elec. mixer until well blended. Gradually increase beating speed to high and whip until mixture will form soft peaks, 4 to 6 minutes. Makes about 3 cups or enough to frost tops and sides of a two-layer or a 13x9-inch cake. Store frosted cake in fridge.

Chocolate frosting: follow the directions above using chocolate Flavor Instant pudding and pie filling.

Buttercream Frosting
Donna Ericson

- 6 T. butter or margarine, softened
- 2 2/3 cup powdered sugar
- 1/2 cup cocoa
- 1/3 cup milk
- 1 t. vanilla

In medium bowl, beat butter. Add powdered sugar and cocoa alternately with milk, beating to spreading consistency (additional milk may be needed). Stir in vanilla. About 2 cups frosting.

Peanut Butter Frosting
Myrna Miller

- 5 tablespoons melted butter
- ¼ c. peanut butter
- 4 tablespoons hot water
- 4 c. powdered sugar
- 3 tablespoons cocoa

Mix butter, peanut butter, and water. Sift sugar and cocoa together and add gradually to first mixture, beating until smooth after each addition. Add more hot water if needed.

Dulce de Leche (Caramel) Sauce
Lyn Olsen

This sauce can be used with anything, put into anything, on top of anything, baked with anything….

Remove label from can of sweetened condensed milk. Place in large saucepan filled with enough water to cover the can. Do not open the can! Heat to boiling with cover on the pan. Reduce heat to medium low and cook for 3 hours. Can must be covered at all times with water while cooking. When done, do not open can until cool. Can add 1 teaspoon salt to the sauce, if desired.

Cream Cheese Filling
Lyn Olsen

Can be used on anything or with anything also….

Beat two 8-ounce packages cream cheese, 1/2 teaspoon lemon juice, 2 cups powdered sugar, 1/2 cup ricotta cheese or cottage cheese, and 1 teaspoon vanilla extract. Beat until fluffy and serve as desired.

Chocolate Frosting
Donna Ericson

6 oz. semi-sweet chocolate, finely chopped
1 8-oz cream cheese, room temp
1/4 cup butter, room temp
1 t. vanilla
2 1/2 cups powdered sugar
2 T. unsweetened cocoa

Melt chocolate in top of double boiler over simmering water, stirring until just melted and smooth. Cool to room temp. Using electric mixer, beat cream cheese, butter and vanilla in large bowl to blend. Beat in powdered sugar in 3 additions, then cooled chocolate and cocoa.

Brown Sugar Icing
Donna Ericson
Good on spice or chocolate cake or whatever.

1 cup powdered sugar
3/4 cup dark brown sugar
1/2 cup whipping cream
1/4 cup (1/2 stick) unsalted butter
1/4 t. vanilla

Sift powdered sugar into med. bowl. Stir brown sugar, whipping cream and butter in med. saucepan over med-lo heat until butter melts and sugar dissolves. Increase heat to med-hi and bring to boil. Boil 3 minutes, occasionally stirring and swirling pan. Remove from heat and stir in vanilla. Pour brown sugar mixture over powdered sugar. Whisk icing until smooth and lightened in color, about 1 minute. Cool icing until lukewarm and icing falls in heavy ribbon from spoon, whisking often, about 15 minutes. Spoon icing to drip down sides of cake. Let stand until icing is firm at least 1 hour.

Oatmeal Cake
Myrna Miller

Absolutely delicious and unique!

Mix well and let stand: 1 cup oatmeal and 1-1/2 cup boiling water.
Cream together ½ cup butter, 1 cup sugar, 1 cup brown sugar.

Add 2 eggs, 1-1/2 cup flour, 1 tsp salt, 1 tsp cinnamon, and 1 tsp vanilla. Add oatmeal mixture. Bake at 350 for 35 minutes.

Frosting for Oatmeal Cake: ½ cup butter, 1 cup brown sugar, 2 cup coconut, ½ cup canned milk, and 1 tsp vanilla. Mix and spread on hot oatmeal cake, broil until light brown.

Wacky Cake
Kathy Agnew

1-1/2 c flour
1 c sugar
3 tablespoons cocoa
½ tsp salt

1 tsp vanilla
1 tsp vinegar
5 tablespoons melted butter
1 c hot water

Sift dry ingredients together in 8x8 baking pan. Make 3 holes in the ingredients. In hole 1 put 1 tsp vanilla, in the second hole 1 tsp vinegar, and in hole 3 melted butter. Pour hot water over all and mix with spoon thoroughly. Bake in same pan for 30 minutes at 350. Frost as desired.

Grandmother's Pound Cake
Lillian Beaulieu

Butter and flour pan and set over to 300. Cream until light and fluffy 1 cup butter, 1-2/3 cup sugar. Beat in one at a time 5 eggs. When creamy fold in 2 cup flour and ¼ tsp salt. Spoon into the pan and bake for 1-1/2 hours.

Texas Sheet Cake
Donna Ericson
Note: bake in 15x10x2" roast pan. Jelly roll pan not deep enough
A superior cake!

In saucepan combine 1 cup water, 1/2 cup butter, 1/4 cup Crisco shortening and 1/4 cup cocoa. Cook and stir till boiling. Remove from heat. In mixer bowl stir together 2 cups flour, 2 cups sugar, 1 t. soda, 1 t. cinnamon, 1/2 t. salt. Add hot cocoa mixture, mix till smooth. Add 1/2 cup buttermilk, 2 eggs, 1 t. vanilla. Beat well. (Note: Add 1 1/2 cups chopped nuts, if desired.) Pour into pan. Bake @ 375 degrees 27 minutes.

During last 5 minutes of baking, prepare frosting:
In saucepan combine 1/2 cup butter, 6 T. (1/3 cup) buttermilk, 1/4 cup cocoa. Cook and stir till boiling, remove from heat. Gradually blend in 4 3/4 cups (1#) powdered sugar and 1 t. vanilla. Beat till smooth. Pour over warm cake. Cool.

I make 2 cakes (separately) and use just one batch of frosting. If I make just one cake, I use 1/2 the frosting and refrigerate the other 1/2 in a covered container for use another time.

Sponge Cake
Myrna Miller

Grease and flour bottoms only of 2 9-inch cake pans. Beat until thick and lemon colored 5 eggs. Beat in gradually 1 cup sugar and beat until thicker. Add 6 tablespoons water and 1 tsp vanilla.

Sift together 1-1/4 cup cake flour, 1-1/4 tsp baking powder, ¼ tsp salt, 14/ tsp cream of tartar. Add to egg mixture. Beat only until smooth and well blended on slow sped. Bake 15 to 20 minutes at 350.

Filling: 1-1/3 c sugar, 3 tablespoon cornstarch, 2 cup liquid drained from cherries, 2 cup red sour pie cherries, ½ tsp red food coloring. Cook sugar, corn starch, and liquid until it thickens. Add cherries and food coloring. Cool before spreading on cake. One hour before serving frost cake with 1 pint whipped cream and top with filling.

Kahlua Chocolate Cake
Donna Ericson

1 pkg. Devil's Food Cake Mix	1 cup Kahlua
4 eggs	3/4 cup vegetable oil
1 cup sour cream	1 (6 oz.) pkg. Semi-sweet Choc. chips

1. Combine cake mix, eggs, sour cream, Kahlua and oil. Beat at low speed to blend. Increase to med/fast speed 3 to 5 minutes. 2. Stir in chocolate chips. 3. Pour into greased and floured 10" bundt or tube pan. Bake at 350 degrees 55 - 60 minutes. Co0l in pan on rack 30 minutes. Loosen, invert, remove, cool completely on rack.

Apple Walnut Cake
Lilian Beaulieu (Very Good)

Grease Bundt pan. Preheat oven to 325 degrees.
1 cup soft butter or margarine
2 cups sugar
3 eggs
3 cups flour
1 1/2 t. soda
1/2 t. salt
1 t. cinnamon
1/4 t. mace
2 t. vanilla
3 cups grated apples
2 cups chopped walnuts

Bake 1 1/2 hours.

Chocolate Pudding Cake
Lyn Olsen
This is the best chocolate cake ever – made it a million times and everyone always loved it the best!

1 c sifted flour
2 teaspoons baking powder
½ teaspoon salt
¾ c sugar
3 tablespoons cocoa
1 teaspoon vanilla

½ cup milk
2 tablespoon melted shortening
½ cup chopped nuts if desired
1-1/2 c. brown sugar, packed
¼ c cocoa
2 cups hot water

Mix flour with baking powder, salt, sugar and 3 tablespoons cocoa. Add vanilla, milk and shortening plus nuts to dry ingredients and stir until well blended. Pour into a 8x8x2 inch pan. Mix brown sugar and cocoa and sprinkle over batter. Pour hot water over entire surface. Bake at 350 degrees for 40-50 minute.

Aunt Clara's Preserves Cake
Aunt Clara

1 pkg yellow cake mix
1 c. raspberry preserves
2 tablespoons orange juice
1 pkg fluffy white frosting mix
½ tsp maple flavoring

Bake cake. Split cake. Mix preserves and orange juice. Spread on top of first layer. Put next top on and prepare frosting by adding maple flavoring to white fluffy frosting mix. Frost top. Heat 475 and bake for 5 minutes.

Custard Cream Filling Boston Cake
Myrna Miller

1/3 c. sugar
½ c. flour
¼ tsp salt
¼ c. milk

1 egg slightly beaten
½ tablespoon butter
1 tsp vanilla

Mix sugar, flour, salt in saucepan. Stir in milk. Cook over low heat, stir until it boils. Boil 1 minute. Remove from heat. Slowly stir in half the hot mixture into beaten egg. Blend into hot mixture in saucepan. Bring to boil. Stir in butter and vanilla. Cool.

Pumpkin Cake Roll
With Cream Cheese Filling
Donna Ericson

Made for Thanksgiving
Everyone loved it and it was easy*

1/3 cup powdered sugar or more (to sprinkle on towel)
Cake:
3/4 cup all-purpose flour
1/2 t. baking powder
1/2 t. baking soda
1/2 t. ground cinnamon

1/2 t. nutmeg
1/2 t. cloves
1/4 t. salt
1 cup sugar
3 large eggs
2/3 cup pumpkin puree
1 cup walnuts, chopped (opt.

FILLING:
8 oz. cream cheese, room temp.,
1 cup powdered sugar

6 T. butter, softened,
1 t. vanilla

1/4 cup powdered sugar (opt) for sprinkling on cake before serving

Preheat oven to 375 degrees. Grease 15x10 inch jelly roll pan; line with wax paper. Grease and flour paper. Sprinkle towel with powdered sugar. Be sure to use plenty so cake won't stick.

Combine flour, baking powder, baking soda and spices in small bowl. Beat eggs and sugar in large mixer bowl until thick. Beat in pumpkin. Stir in flour mixture. Spread evenly into prepared pan. Sprinkle with nuts.

Bake for 14 minutes or until top of cake springs back when touched. Immediately loosen and turn cake onto prepared towel. Carefully peel off paper. Roll up cake and towel together, starting with narrow end. Cool on wire rack.

Beat cream cheese, powdered sugar, butter and vanilla in small mixer bowl until smooth. Carefully unroll cake; remove towel. Spread cream cheese mixture over cake. Reroll cake. Wrap in plastic wrap and refrigerate at least one hour. Sprinkle with powdered sugar before serving if desired.

Note: 1 sm can pumpkin makes 2 rolls, 1 large can makes 5.

Hints: I find that if I use parchment, I don't have to grease or flour the pan. I just spray the pan so the parchment stays in place; it peels off the cake just fine.. Also, I use the small mixer bowl for beating the eggs and sugar and blend the flour and spices in to the same bowl. I made 5 rolls today and did the following: measured and sifted all the dry ingredients for each roll and put that into 5 of my large wooden salad bowls, put 2/3 cup pumpkin into each of 5 small sauce dishes, beat the butter and eggs till thick, added the pumpkin, then slowly added the flour. That seemed to work very well for me.

My aunt worked for more than 55 years at the same job at Hennessy's Department Store as the advertising manager. I remember many a day after school slipping up the stairs to the mezzanine and sneaking behind all of the displays into a small crowded corner room where my aunt worked. She kept drawerfuls of prior artwork and would make copies of these as needed to create new ads. She typed the copy on an old black typewriter which strikingly resembled Angela Lansbury in "Murder She Wrote." She would then take this copy to the newspaper after she made corrections and there we children could watch them setting the paper.

Oftentimes, I would hurry after high school to her office so that I could go on breaks with her to Gamer's.

Gamer's Mocha Cake

Donna Ericson (Gamer's was a historical restaurant in Butte's Uptown Main Street - it was "the" place to do lunch)

1 cup brown sugar
1 t. soda
1/2 cup white sugar
pinch salt
1/2 cup Crisco shortening
2 eggs
2 heap. T. cocoa
1 cup sour milk or buttermilk
2 cups flour
1 cup nuts
1 cup raisins

Cream sugars and shortening. Add beaten eggs. Alternately add sifted dry ingredients with sour milk. Then add nuts and raisins and bake at 375 degrees.

Frosting:
   1 pkg. Kraft Caramels. Melt over hot water. Add 2 T. heavy cream. Add powdered sugar to spreading consistency.   Add the following:
   1/4 to 1/2 cup cream cheese
   2 T. butter
   1 t. vanilla
Beat together.

Rice Krispies Brownies

Lyn Olsen

You can never fail with these – everyone loves them!

Bake any brownie recipe, then cover with the following when cool. First frost brownies with a thin layer of white frosting. On stove top melt several 2 tablespoons of butter with a 1 cup of peanut butter and 1 cup of chocolate chips. When melted, add several cups of rice krispies and spread on top of brownies and white frosting.

Devil's Food Pound Cake
Donna Ericson
High altitude directions below.

1 pkg. Duncan Hines Moist Deluxe Devil's Food Cake Mix
1 sm. pkg. chocolate instant pudding and pie filling mix
4 eggs
1 1/4 cups water
1/2 cup oil

Glaze: 1/2 cup Duncan Hines Creamy Homestyle Frosting (favorite flavor).

Preheat oven to 350 degrees. Grease and flour 10 inch Bundt pan or tube pan.

Combine cake mix, pudding mix, eggs, water and oil in large bowl. Beat at medium speed with electric mixer for 2 minutes. Pour into pan. Bake for 50 - 60 minutes or until toothpick inserted in center comes out clean. Cool in pan 25 minutes. Invert onto serving plate. Cool Completely.

For glaze, heat frosting in small saucepan over medium heat, stirring constantly, until thin, or microwave on high 10 to 15 seconds. Do not overheat. Drizzle over cake.

Tip: Cake can also be made in two prepared loaf pans. Bake at 350 for 50-55 minutes for 9x5x4 1/2" pans or 55-60 minutes for 8 1/2 x 4 1/2" pans or until toothpick inserted in center comes out clean. Cool 15 minutes before removing from pan.

High altitudes: Preheat oven to 375. Stir 1/3 cup flour into mix. Combine as directed using 4 eggs, 1 1/2 cups water and 1/3 cup oil. Bake in 10 inch bundt pan or tube pan for 50-55 minutes.

White Cake
Lyn Olsen

I remember my friend from a long time ago made this and it was the best cake ever!

Sift together 3 cups sifted cake flour, 1 tsp baking powder and ½ tsp salt. Set aside.

Cream together until smooth: 1 cup butter and 1 tsp vanilla. Gradually add 1 cup of sugar, beating until fluffy. Set aside.

Beat until frothy 6 egg whites. Add gradually several tablespoons of sugar and beat well, until ¾ c. sugar has been added. Beat until rounded peaks are formed.

To the cream mixture, add alternatively small portions of dry ingredients in addition to ½ cup water and ½ c. milk. (Do not overbeat). Spread beaten egg whites over this batter and gently fold together. Turn into greased and floured cake pans. Bake at 350 for 30 to 35 minutes until cake springs bake when touch lightly.

Carrot Cake
Lyn Olsen

3 c. flour
2 c. sugar
2 tsp baking powder
2 tsp cinnamon
1-1/2 c. oil

2 c carrots shredded
1-1/2 c. nuts
1 small can pineapple
3 eggs
2 tsp vanilla

Mix dry ingredients. Add remaining ingredients in order. Mix and pour into greased and floured cake pan. Bake at 350 for 30 to 35 minutes.

Cream cheese Frosting: ¼ pound butter, 1 t. vanilla, 2-1/3 c. powdered sugar, and one 8 oz cream cheese whipped until fluffy.

Chocolate Zucchini Cake
Donna Ericson

Cake:
2 1/2 cups unsifted flour
1/2 cup unsweetened cocoa
2 1/2 t. baking powder
1 1/2 t. soda
1 t. salt
1 t. cinnamon
3/4 cup butter or margarine
2 cups sugar
3 eggs
2 cups grated unpeeled zucchini
2 t. grated orange peel
2 t. vanilla
1/2 cup milk
1 cup chopped walnuts

Glaze:
3/4 cup powdered sugar
1 T. orange juice
1/2 t. grated orange peel

Generously grease a 12-cup Bundt pan; set aside. Preheat oven to 350.

In medium bowl, combine first 6 ingredients; set aside. In large mixer bowl with mixer at medium speed beat butter or margarine and sugar until light and fluffy. Add eggs and continue beating until well mixed. Stir in zucchini, orange and vanilla. Alternately stir in dry ingredients, milk and nuts. Pour into greased pan. Bake for 1 hour or until toothpick inserted in center comes out clean. Let cool in pan on wire rack 25 minutes. Invert to remove. Spread with orange glaze while cake is still warm.

Orange Glaze: In small bowl, combine powdered sugar, orange juice and peel; stir until smooth.

Cradle Cake
Lyn Olsen

This cake is superb – you should have this cake at least once in your life!

2 c. flour
1 tablespoon baking powder
½ tsp salt
4 eggs, separated at room temperature
2 c. sugar divided
2 squares semisweet chocolate melted with 3 tablespoons water

1 c. chopped nuts (pecans or walnuts)
1 square unsweetened chocolate (1 oz)
½ c butter softened
1 tsp vanilla
¾ c. milk

Great 9 or 10 inch tube pan. Line bottom with waxed paper, set aside. Stir together flour, baking powder and salt, set aside. In medium bowl beat egg whites until soft peaks form. Gradually beat in 1 c. sugar until stiff, glossy peaks form. Fold in nuts and grated chocolate. Spread mixture on bottom and up ¾ of the way on the pan as though lining it. In large bowl cream butter and remaining 1 c sugar until light and fluffy. Beat in egg yolks and vanilla until well blended. Stir in flour mixture alternatively with milk until well blended. Pour cake mixture into pan, making sure it is surrounded by meringue on all sides and lower than top of meringue. Bake at 325 65 to 75 minutes or until pick inserted in middle of cake comes out clean. Do not invert pan. Cool on rack 25 minute or until sides can be touched. Run knife on the inside of the cake along the cake pan to loosen it and turn onto serving plate.

Pumpkin Dump Cake
Devvi Morgan

1 - 29oz. can pumpkin puree
1 - 12oz. can evaporated milk
3 eggs
1 cup sugar
1 t. salt

3 t. cinnamon

1 box yellow cake mix
1 cup chopped pecans
3/4 cup melted butter

Preheat oven to 350 degrees.
Mix 1st 6 ingredients until well blended. Pour batter into 9x13 inch greased pan. Sprinkle cake mix on top and then cover with pecans. Pour melted butter over top. Bake 50 minutes. Top with whipped cream if desired. Serve either warm or chilled. Store in refrigerator.

Carrot Cake
Donna Ericson (recipe from Betty Maki, Donna's best friend from across the street)

Beat together:
   1 1/2 cups sugar
   1 1/2 cups oil
   4 large eggs
   1 t. vanilla
Add:
   2 cups flour
   1 t. baking soda
   2 t. cinnamon

Fold in:
   1 cup crushed pineapple with juice
   3 cups grated carrots
   1 cup chopped nuts

Bake in 13x9x2" pan, @ 350 degrees for 40 minutes or until done.

Frosting:
   1 1/2 cups powdered sugar
   1/4 to 1/2 cup cream cheese
   2 T. butter
   1 t. vanilla
Beat together.

Tiramisu
Donna Ericson (quilting friend Donna Colvin)

6 egg yolks
1/4 c. sugar
1 1/4 c. mascarpone cheese*
1 3/4 c. whipping cream
1/2 c. brandy liqueur or
2 3oz. pkgs. lady fingers**
   brandied espresso***
grated semi-sweet chocolate or unsweetened cocoa powder

*Substitute - 8 oz. cream cheese, 1/4 c. sour cream and 2 T. whipping cream blended together. Mascarpone is a triple cream cheese imported from Italy, very hard to find and expensive.

**Betty Crocker pound cake made without the added butter seems to work as well or better instead of the lady fingers.

***If you don't have an espresso maker, strong instant coffee can be substituted; flavor either with brandy or brandy flavoring or rum.

In a bowl beat egg yolks and sugar over a pan of boiling water until thick and lemon colored, beating constantly until cooked about 8 - 10 minutes. Remove from heat, add madcarpone cheese or substitution and blend well. Whip cream until stiff peaks form, fold into egg yolk mixture, set aside.

Line bottom of 2 1/2 to 3 quart bowl or other dish with cake that has been sliced into 1/4" slices dipped very quickly into the espresso. Cover with a layer of the cream mixture, then repeat with more cake and cream until used up. Garnish with grated chocolate.

Another version
(Donna Ericson)

3 c. pound cake cubes (1/2")
1 small pkg. instant vanilla pudding mix
2 env. Maxwell House Cappuccino,
2 c. cold milk, divided
Amaretto Flavor, divided
8 oz. Phil. Cream cheese, divided
2 c. thawed Cool Whip

Cover bottom of 8" sq. dish with cake. Dissolve 1 envelope of the cappuccino in 1/2 c. of the milk; sprinkle over cake. Beat cream cheese in large bowl with electric mixer until smooth. Gradually beat in remaining 1 1/2 c. milk until smooth. Add pudding mix and remaining envelope of cappuccino. Beat on low speed until blended. Stir in Cool Whip. Spoon over cake. Refrigerate 3 hrs. Makes 6 servings.

COOKIES

Pumpkin Cheesecake Bars
Donna Ericson (from neighbor across alley - John Joy)

1 16oz. pkg. pound cake mix
3 eggs
2 T. butter, melted
4 t. pumpkin pie spice
1 8 oz. pkg. cream cheese, softened
1 can Eagle Brand sweetened condensed milk
1 16 oz. can pumpkin
1/2 t. salt
1 cup chopped nuts

Preheat oven to 350. In large mixer bowl on low speed, combine cake mix, 1 egg, butter and 2 tsp. pumpkin pie spice, until crumbly. Press onto bottom of 15" jelly roll pan. In large mixer bowl, beat cheese until fluffy. Gradually beat in Eagle Brand milk, then remaining 2 eggs, pumpkin, remaining 2 t. pumpkin pie spice and salt. Mix well. Pour over crust, sprinkle with nuts. Bake 30 - 35 minutes or until set. Cool. Chill, cut into bars. Store covered.

Grandma Miller's Soft Chocolate Cookies
Donna Ericson

1 cup Crisco shortening
4 cups flour
2 cups brown sugar
3 t. soda
2 eggs
1 1/2 cups milk
3-4 sqs. melted choc.
1 cup chopped nuts
1 cup raisins, optional

Bake at 375 degrees for 11 minutes. Very good with easy caramel icing.

Ranger Cookies
Michelle Hunt

1 c. white sugar
1 c. brown sugar
2 eggs
1 c. butter
½ tsp baking powder
1 tsp salt

2 c. flour
1 tsp vanilla
2 c. oatmeal
1 package semisweet chocolate chips
(can omit oatmeal and put in coconut instead).

Cream sugar, eggs and butter. Add sifted dry ingredients. Beat adding the vanilla until all of the ingredients are blended. Add oatmeal and chocolate chips and bake at 350 for 10 to 15 minutes.

Sugar Cookies

1-1/2 cups soft butter
2 c white sugar
4 eggs

1 tsp vanilla
5 c flour
1 tsp salt

Cream butter and sugar together. Add vanilla and eggs and beat until smooth. Add salt to 2 c flour, stir and add to creamed mixture and mix. Add 2 more cups of flour and stir to mix. Add one more cup of flour and mix. Take portion and roll out, cut our shapes and put on cookie tray. Put sprinkles or anything else desired on top. Bake at 375 until light golden brown, about 12 minutes.

Cocoa Oatmeal Cookies
Myrna Miller

For some reason, these chocolate oatmeal cookies are unlike any other and were always our favorite growing up, as well as everyone else later who had the pleasure of them.

2-1/2 c. flour
1 tsp baking powder
1 tsp salt
2/3 c. cocoa
2-1/2 c sugar
2 eggs beaten
1 c. milk
3 tsp vanilla
2/3 c Crisco shortening melted
2/3 c. butter melted
4 c. rolled oats

Sift dry ingredients (flour, baking powder, salt, cocoa, sugar). Combine egg, milk, and vanilla to dry ingredients. Stir in rolled oats and drop by teaspoon onto cookie sheet and bake at 350 for 15 to 20 minutes. Makes 5 dozen.

Billie Jean King's Giant Polka Dot Cookies
Michelle Hunt

Made these a million times and everyone always loved them!

½ c. butter
½ c. sugar
½ c. brown sugar
½ tsp vanilla
1 egg
1 c. flour
½ tsp salt
1 c. oatmeal
1 pkg M&M

Thoroughly cream sugars, butter and vanilla. Beat in eggs. Sift together flour and salt and add to creamed mixture, blending well. Stir in rolled oats, spread large tablespoon of dough on cookie sheet and press down, then put M&M on top. Bake at 375 for 12 to 14 minutes.

Neiman's $250.00 Cookies
Lyn Olsen

This recipe has been around a long time and it is said that a woman paid $250 for the recipe because she thought that it was going to cost her $2.50, but it is a fantastic cookie that everyone loves and I made for many years.

2. c. butter	3-1/4 c flour
2 c. brown sugar	5 cups oatmeal blended in a blender
2 c. sugar	1 tsp salt
4 eggs	1 – 8 oz grated Hershey bar
2 tsp vanilla	3 c. chopped nuts if desired
2 tsp baking powder	24 oz semisweet chocolate chips

Cream butter and sugars. Add eggs and vanilla. Mix together with flour, oatmeal, salt, baking powder. Add chips, grated chocolate bar and nuts. Refrigerate if desired, then drop by teaspoonful onto baking sheets and bake at 375 for 6 minutes. Makes 112 cookies.

Bon Bon Cookies
Myrna Miller

½ c soft butter	1-1/2 c flour
¾ c. sifted powdered sugar	1/8 tsp salt
1 tablespoon vanilla	1 square unsweetened chocolate melted

Mix butter, sugar, vanilla, and chocolate. Blend in flour and salt by hand. Drop by spoonful onto cookie sheet and bake at 350 for 12 minutes. Dip tops of warm cookies in icing. Icing: Mix 1 c sifted powdered sugar with ¼ cup cream, 1 tsp vanilla and 1 square melted chocolate.

Blarney Stones
Pat Wilson (Pat was the owner and manager of the Ranchhouse bar in uptown Butte for many years which was notorious for awesome pizza!

2 eggs	1 teaspoon baking powder
1 c. sugar	1 teaspoon salt
½ c. hot water	1 teaspoon vanilla
1 c. cake flour	

Mix flour, sugar, baking powder, and salt. Blend. Add beaten eggs, beathing while adding eggs. Slowly add boiling water beating the entire time. Add vanilla. Put in a 9 inch pan (greased lightly). Bake for 20 minutes at 375 degrees and cut into squares.

Make powdered sugar frosting by using Crisco shortening, margarine or butter and adding powdered sugar until spreadable consistency. Spread frosting on all side of the squares of cake and then roll in ground salted peanuts.

Date Nut Drops
Devvi Morgan
Delicious & Soft

2 cups chopped dates, about 1/2 # *	3 eggs
1/2 cup sugar *	1 t. vanilla
1/2 cup water *	4 cups flour
===============	1 t. soda
1 cup butter	1 t. salt
1 cup sugar	1 t. cinnamon
1 cup brown sugar, firmly packed	1 1/2 cups chopped nuts

Combine dates, 1/2 cup sugar and water in saucepan. Cook, stirring occasionally, until mixture is the consistency of very thick jam. Cool.

Cream butter, add sugars gradually, beating until light and fluffy. Beat in eggs and vanilla. Stir together dry ingredients. Add to creamed mixture, blending thoroughly. Stir in nuts and date mixture.

Drop by rounded teaspoonfuls about 2" apart onto greased baking sheet. Bake in a moderate oven (375 degrees) 12-15 minutes. Remove cookies and cool on racks. Makes 12 dozen.

* Note: You can use 2 1/2 cups mincemeat instead of these three ingredients.

Chocolate Drop Cookies
Myrna Miller

1-1/3 c. flour	2 squares unsweetened chocolate
½ tsp baking powder	½ c sour milk
¼ tsp salt	1 tsp vanilla
½ c butter	½ c nuts if desired
1 beaten egg	1 c. brown sugar

Cream butter and sugar, and vanilla. Add eggs and chocolate and beat well. Sift flour, baking powder, and salt and add to other mixture alternately with milk. Add nuts. Drop by spoonful onto cookie sheet and bake for 10 minutes. Prepare frosting using 1-1/2 c. powdered sugar, ¼ cup cocoa, 2 tablespoons melted butter, ½ tsp vanilla and enough hot water to make it spreadable. Put on cookies while warm.

Chocolate Peanut Butter Bars
Lyn Olsen

Absolutely delicious, like a reese's…

1 c. peanut butter
1 c. soft butter
3 c. powdered sugar
16 whole graham crackers crushed

Mix well until like pie crust dough. Press firmly in 8x8 or 9x9 pan. Melt 12 oz chocolate chips and pour over the top.

Jubilee Jumbles
Myrna Miller

Unforgettably the best!

Cream together:
½ c. butter
1 c. brown sugar
½ c. sugar
2 eggs

Add:
1 c. evaporated milk
1 tsp vanilla

Mixed together and then add:
2-3/4 c. flour
1 teaspoon salt

Add 1 c. coconut

Dough will be looser than most cookie doughs so that is okay. Chill briefly and then drop by spoonful onto cookie sheet and bake at 350 degrees until golden brown.

After cookies are baked, be ready to frost with following recipe: 2 tablespoons butter and cook until brown. Take off heat and then beat 2 c. powdered sugar into the butter with ¼ c. evaporated milk. Frost each cookie with this frosting which should run a little on the sides of the cookies.

Graham Crackers
Vickie Danton

4 c. flour
1 c. butter
1 c. brown sugar

1 tsp cream of tartar
1 egg, lightly beaten
½ c. hot water

Preheat oven to 350. Cut in butter until mixture is like coarse oatmeal. Add remaining ingredients and enough water to make dough that can be rolled like pastry. Cut into shapes with cookie cutters and bake for 15 to 20 minutes.

Potato Chip Cookies
Donna Ericson

16 T. butter
3/4 c. sugar
1 1/2 c. flour
1 t. vanilla

1 c. crushed potato chips
1 c. ch. pecans
Powdered sugar

Cream together butter and sugar. Gradually add flour and mix well. Add vanilla and potato chips and mix well. Fold in nuts.

Drop onto ungreased cookie sheets and flatten with bottom of a drinking glass which has been dipped in sugar.

Bake at 350 degrees 8-10 minutes. 3 or 4 dozen.

another version of potato chip cookies, just as good...
Potato Chip Cookies

Preheat oven to 350 degrees

1# butter
1 cup sugar
1 t. vanilla

3 1/2 cups flour
2 cups crushed potato chips (4 1/2 oz.)
1/2 cup chopped pecans

Cream butter and sugar and vanilla and stir in flour. Add chips and nuts. Drop by tsp. onto sheet, close together.....won't spread.

Bake 15 minutes.

6 Layer Cookies
Myrna Miller

Everyone has a version of these and you could put anything you want in.

¼ pound butter
1 c graham cracker crumbs
1 c shredded coconut
1 12-oz pkg Chocolate Chips
1 12-oz pkg Butterscotch Chips
1 14-oz can sweetened condensed milk
1 c chopped walnuts

Heat oven to 350. Place butter in a 13x9 and melt over moderate heat. Sprinkle graham cracker crumbs in an even layer over the melted butter. Sprinkle coconut over crumbs, then sprinkle chocolate pieces over the this, then butterscotch chps. Pour condensed milk over the entire mixture and add chopped nuts on top. Bake 30 to 35 minutes. Cook and cut into bars.

Unbaked Chocolate Oatmeal Drops
Myrna Miller

Combine in a saucepan: 2 c sugar, ½ c. milk, ½ c butter. Boil 1 minute, stirring constantly. Pour over 3 c oatmeal and ½ c cocoa. Stir in 1 cup chopped nuts or coconut if desired. Drop by spoonful onto waxed paper and let cool.

Monster Cookies
Donna Ericson

Mix whole batch in blue roaster
Huge batch - can easily be cut in half

Oven: 350 degrees   12 minutes   Yield: 20 dozen

Cream well: 4 cups sugar
    2# brown sugar
    2 cups butter
    3# peanut butter
Add and mix well:
    12 eggs, beaten
    1 T. vanilla
    1 T. light Karo

Add: 18 cups quick oatmeal
    8 t. soda
    1# chocolate chips or raisins
    1# M & M candies

Drop on greased cookie sheet with small ice cream scoop. Flatten with fork. Bake at 350.

Chocolate Chip Cookies
Myrna Miller

Mom liked the chocolate chip cookies to have more flour than usual and then she would roll them into balls as well as not cooking them long.

2-1/4 c. flour	1 t vanilla
1 teaspoon salt	2 eggs
1 c. butter	1 16 oz bag of chocolate chips
¾ c. sugar	Add nuts if desired
¾ c. brown sugar	

Cream butter and sugars. Add vanilla and eggs and beat well. Add flour and salt and beat. Add more flour if desired until consistency desired. Drop onto cookie sheet by spoonful and bake at 350 degrees until desired, approximately 10 minutes until golden brown or less if it is desired that cookies are gooey in the middle.

Brownies
Myrna Miller

Been making these since a small kid with my mom –everyone loves brownies!

2 c. sugar	1 c. milk
½ c butter	1-1/3 c. flour
2 squares unsweetened chocolate	½ tsp baking powder
4 eggs	½ tsp salt
1 tsp vanilla	1 c. chopped nuts if desired

Cream sugar and butter. Add eggs and melted chocolate and vanilla. Add milk alternately with dry ingredients. Add nuts and bake at 375 for 35 minutes.

Spritz
Devvi Morgan

1 cup butter	2 1/3 cups flour
1 cup sugar	1/2 t. baking powder
1 egg	1/4 t. salt
1 t. vanilla or 1/2 t. almond extract	

Cream butter and sugar, blend in eggs and flavoring. Combine dry ingredients, stir into creamed mixture. Mix well. Do not chill dough. Pack dough, 1/2 at a time, in cookie gun. Press into desired shapes on ungreased cookie sheet. If desired, sprinkle with desired sugar crystals or trim with pieces red and green candied cherries, pressing cherries lightly into dough. Bake at 400 degrees for 7 - 8 minutes. Cool. Makes 6 dozen.

Snorkels
Donna Ericson
(Ruth Piper 12/1966)

1# Blue Bonnet Margarine
4 cups flour

Mix like pie crust. Blend in 16 oz. dry cottage cheese. Chill. Divide into 12 equal balls. Roll out each pie shaped. Brush with melted butter and sprinkle with cinnamon, finely chopped nuts and sugar. Then cut into 8 wedges.

Roll each wedge from outside to center. Put on cookie sheet. Bake at 375 degrees 25 minutes.

Frost (while still warm) with vanilla powdered sugar frosting.

Chewy Oatmeal Cookie
Donna Ericson

Ingredients:
3/4 c. Butter Flavor Crisco shortening
1 c. flour
1 1/4 c. packed brown sugar
1/2 t. soda
1 egg
1/4 t. salt

1/3 c. milk
1/4 t. cinnamon
1 1/2 t. vanilla
1 c. raisins
3 c. quick oats
1 c. ch. nuts

Heat oven to 375* Combine Crisco shortening, brown sugar, egg, milk and vanilla in large bowl. Beat at medium speed of electric mixer until well blended. Combine oats, flour, baking soda, salt and cinnamon. Mix into creamed mixture at low speed just until blended. Stir in raisins and nuts. Drop rounded tablespoonfuls of dough 2 inches apart onto baking sheet. Bake 10 - 12 minutes, or until lightly browned. Cool 2 minutes on baking sheet. Remove to rack to cool.

Variations: Half-dipped--omit raisins and nuts. Bake and cool. Microwave 1 cup Duncan Hines Dutch Fudge Frosting for 20-25 seconds, or until smooth and thin. Dip top half of cookie in frosting. Lay on waxed paper until set. Favorite chip cookies--omit raisins and nuts. Add 1 cup baking chips to batter.

Mexican Wedding Balls
Donna Ericson

Preheat oven to 375 degrees.

1# real butter
1 cup powdered sugar
4 cups flour
2 tsp. vanilla
1 1/2 cups chopped pecans (6 oz.)

Cream butter and sugar. Add vanilla and flour. Mix well and add nuts. Roll either into balls or sticks and bake till light brown (9 to 11 minutes.) Roll immediately in powdered sugar and again when cool.

Crisco Ultimate Chocolate Chip Cookies
Donna Ericson

1 1/2 cups butter flavored Crisco shortening
2 1/2 cups brown sugar
4 T. milk
2 T. vanilla
2 eggs

3 1/2 cups flour
2 t. salt
1 1/2 t. soda
2 cups choc. chips
2 cups pecan pieces

Heat oven to 375. Cream Crisco shortening, brown sugar, milk and vanilla in large bowl. Blend until creamy. Blend in eggs. Combine flour, salt and baking soda. Add to creamed mixture, gradually. Stir in chocolate chips and nuts. Drop rounded tablespoonfuls of dough 3 inches apart on ungreased baking sheet. Bake 8-10 minutes for chewy cookies (they will look light and moist.....do not overbake) or 11 - 13 minutes for crisp cookies. Cool on baking sheet 2 minutes. Remove to cooling rack. 6 dozen 3" cookies. Note: If nuts are omitted, use 1 1/2 cups semi-sweet chocolate chips.

Rum Balls
Myrna Miller (never a Christmas was to be had without these!)

Melt 1 pkg. choc. chips in double boiler. Add 3 T. white Karo, 1 pkg. powdered sugar, 1 cup finely chopped walnuts, 1 3/4 cups finely ground vanilla wafers, 1/3 or more cup rum. Form into balls and roll in powdered sugar.

Donna's Soft Raisin Cookies

1 cup water
2 cups raisins
1 cup shortening
2 eggs lightly beaten
1 tsp. vanilla
3-½ cups flour
1 tsp baking powder

1 tsp baking soda
1 tsp salt
½ tsp cinnamon
½ tsp nutmeg
½ cup chopped walnuts
1-¾ cups sugar

Combine raisins and water in a small saucepan and bring to a boil. Cook for 3 minutes, remove from the heat and let cool (do not drain). In a mixing bowl, cream shortening gradually, add sugar. Add eggs and vanilla. Stir in nuts and raisins. Combine dry ingredients and add to above mixture and blend thoroughly. Drop by teaspoonfuls 2 inches apart on greased baking sheets. Bake at 375 degrees 10-12 minutes. Yield: about 6 dozen

Mrs. Leskovar's Special K Squares
Donna Ericson
Delicious

Heat in large saucepan (do not boil)
   1 cup peanut butter
   1 cup white sugar
   1 cup white Karo syrup
   1/3 cup honey

Pour over 6 cups of Special K or Rice Krispies (use Special K) in large bowl.
Press into greased 9 x 12 pan.
Melt 1 12 oz. pkg. semi-sweet choc. chips (2 cups) and 1 6 oz. butterscotch chips (1 cup).
Spread on top of cereal mixture. Put in fridge 25-30 minutes. TIME THEM!
Cut into 1" squares. Put back in fridge and time them again for 25 - 30 minutes. Enjoy!

Lace Cookies
Donna Ericson

To keep these delicate cookies crisp and crunchy, store in refrigerator.

Preheat oven to 350 degrees.

1/2 cup flour
2/3 cup (3 oz.) finely ground raw unsalted cashews
1/3 cup firmly packed light brown sugar

1/4 cup light Karo
1/4 cup butter
2 T. milk

Line 2 cookie sheets with foil; set aside. In a small bowl combine flour and cashews. In a 2 quart saucepan heat light brown sugar, Karo, butter and milk, stirring constantly, over medium heat until mixture begins to boil. Remove from heat; gradually add dry ingredients; stir until moistened.

Drop batter by heaping teaspoonfuls at least 3 inches apart onto foil-lined cookie sheets. Bake 10 to 12 minutes or until golden brown. Slide foil from cookie sheets to wire racks to cook for about 5 minutes. Then carefully remove cookies from foil. Reline cookie sheets with foil and continue making more cookies until batter is used. Let cookies cool completely on wire racks. When cool, store in tightly covered container with waxed paper between the layers; refrigerate up to 1 week. Makes about 2 1/2 to 3 dozen.

Cocoa Refrigerated Cookies
Myrna Miller

One of us kids all-time Christmas favorite which mom made every Christmas.

2 c. flour sifted
1/3 cup cocoa
1 tsp baking powder
¼ tsp salt
2/3 c butter

1 c sugar
1 egg
½ tsp vanilla
3 tablespoons milk

Sift dry ingredients. Cream butter and sugars. Beat in eggs and milk. Add flour mixture. Separate into 2 balls and roll out into rolls measuring 1-2/ inches in diameter. Wrap in wax paper and chill for 5 to 6 hours. Cut in slices 1/8 inch thick and placed on cookie sheet. Bake at 350 for 15 minutes.

Date Filled Cookies
Lilian Bealieu – one of our Christmas favorites!

1 cup shortening
3 2/3 cup flour
2 cups brown sugar
1 t. salt
2 eggs
1 t. baking powder
1/3 cup milk
1 t. vanilla
date filling

Cream shortening. Add brown sugar, gradually, then slightly beaten eggs. Stir in milk and vanilla. Sift dry ingredients and add. Drop by t. onto un-greased baking sheet, leaving room to spread, about 2" apart. Center 1/2 t. filling on dough, then another 1/2 t. dough. Bake at 375 degrees 10 minutes. 5 dozen.

Date nut filling:
   1 1/2 cups or 1/2# dates, pitted and chopped, 2/3 cup sugar, 2/3 cup water, 1 T. lemon juice, 1/2 cup nuts. Combine dates, sugar and water. Cook and stir until thick. Remove from heat. Add lemon juice and nuts. Cool

Giant Snickerdoodles
Donna Ericson
Preheat oven to 375 degrees.

1 cup (1/2#) butter
1 1/2 cups + 2 T. sugar
2 eggs
2 3/4 cups flour

2 t. cream of tartar
1 t. soda
1/4 t. salt
2 t. cinnamon

In large mixer bowl with electric mixer at med. speed, cream butter, 1 1/2 cups sugar and eggs until light and fluffy, scraping sides of bowl occasionally. In a separate bowl, combine flour, cream of tartar, baking soda and salt. Add to creamed mixture until well blended. Refrigerate dough for 30 minutes. Combine remaining 2 T. sugar and cinnamon in a flat open bowl. Shape dough into 2-inch balls and roll in cinnamon-sugar. Place 3 inches apart on ungreased cookie sheets. Bake 12 - 15 minutes until golden brown. (Snickerdoodles will puff up at first, then flatten out during baking.) Remove from cookie sheet and cool on wire rack. Makes 2 dozen cookies. To freeze: Wrap well, label and date. Freeze up to 3 months.

Coconut Pecan Squares

Donna Ericson (December 19, 1958) I remember mom making these and they are AWESOME!

Cream ½ cup butter with ½ cup brown sugar. Add 1 cup flour and mix well. Press into greased 8x8 pan spreading batter evenly into corners. Bake at 350 for 20 minutes. Meanwhile, eat 2 eggs til frothy. Gradually add 1 cup brown sugar and beat til thick. Add 1 cup chopped pecans and ½ cup shredded coconut which has been tossed with 2 tablespoons flour. Add 1 tsp vanilla and pinch salt. Mix well. Spread over baked and cooled crust. Bake 20 minute more at 350 or until well browned. Sprinkle with confectioners sugar when cool and cut into 1 inch squares.

Chinese Chews

Myrna Miller

In heavy saucepan combine large pkg. chocolate chips and large pkg. butterscotch chips. Melt, stirring constantly over low heat. Remove from heat and stir in approximately 6 oz. La Choy Chow Mein noodles. Add 1 1/2 cups cashews or peanuts. Mix quickly to coat each noodle.

Drop by tablespoonfuls onto wax paper. Cool.

OTHER DESSERTS

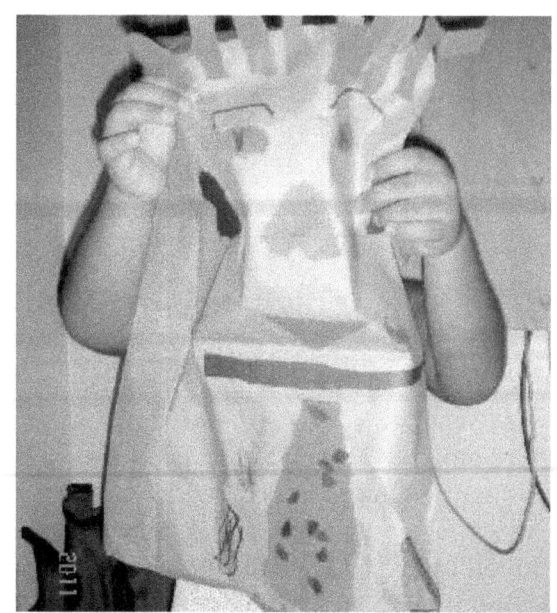

Halloween was a treat for us because we got little candy other than at this time of the year. As a kid, our Halloween costumes consisted of a brown paper grocery bag. We would decorate the bags in grade school and there were competitions for the best decorated. We would cut out eyes and a mouth and decorate it with anything available.

In those days, the favorite Halloween treat was oftentimes homemade popcorn balls for homemade treats were acceptable then.

mommytots.com

Popcorn balls
Donna Ericson
(Candy Popcorn) Todd's Favorite

Cook on right front burner of new stove on #4. Use pressure cooker or deep saucepan for syrup as it really boils up.

2 cups sugar
2/3 cup light Karo
2/3 cup butter
1 1/2 t. salt

2/3 cup water
3 t. vanilla
food coloring (opt)
7 quarts warm popcorn *

Boil until nearly brittle (270 degrees here in Butte, 278 degrees elsewhere) when tested in cold water. Takes about 35 minutes.   Add 3t. vanilla and coloring, if desired. Pour over 7 quarts warm popcorn and mix well with spoon. Dip hands in cold water, shake well and shape into balls. Wrap in wax paper. If making candy popcorn, just dump popcorn covered with syrup onto clean kitchen cupboard and spread out to cool. Store in airtight container. Note: If desired, substitute 3t. almond flavoring or 3t. anise flavoring for vanilla.

When Halloween came, we would don our decorated brown garbage bags and go out in search of even the smallest piece of candy from the houses within our neighborhood and as far as we could walk on the very dark and mostly very cold nights; many a times we struggled in the ever-increasing deep snow as it continued to snow all night.

Rice Pudding
Lyn Olsen

There is a very quick way to make a dish similar to rice pudding which we lived off of oftentimes as kids, this and bread with butter and sugar on it, or else cheerios cooked in butter and sugar - or you can make the legitimate recipe which is always one of my most favorite desserts. QUICK WAY: Cook rice. When done, put several big spoonfuls of rice into a bowl, add sugar, cinnamon and milk as desired and heat.

REAL RECIPE:

1-1/2 c. cooked rice	½ tsp salt
¾ c. sugar	½ tsp cinnamon or allspice
¾ c. milk	1 tablespoon butter
3 eggs	1 tsp vanilla
½ tsp baking powder	

Put rice in baking dish 7x7. Add sugar gradually beating in between additions. Add eggs, beating well after each egg. Add dry ingredients, butter and vanilla. Bake at 300 for 30 minutes.

Old Fashioned Rice Pudding
Myrna Miller

Put in casserole:	½ tsp salt
4 c milk	1 tsp vanilla
¼ c uncooked rice	

Bake uncovered for 3 hours at 300. During the first hour stir 3 times with fork so that the rice will not settle, add two eggs before 30 minute of end of cooking time for richer pudding. Can also add raisins.

Forgotten Meringues
Lyn Olsen

6 egg whites, ½ teaspoon cream of tartar, 2 cup sugar.
 Heat oven to 400 degrees. Beat egg whites with lemon juice or cream of tartar until frothy. Gradually beat in sugar a little at a time. Beat until stiff and glossy. Drop by small spoonfuls in circles on brown paper on sheet. Put into oven, close door, turn off oven and let stand over night.

Chocolate Mousse
Myrna Miller

Cook over low heat or in a double boiler, stirring frequently: 1 cup of milk, 2 oz unsweetened chocolate or 3 tablespoons unsweetened powder chocolate and 1 tablespoon melted butter, ¼ cup sugar, 1 teaspoon gelatin. When done, beat until smooth and well blended. Chill until thick. Then add 1 teaspoon vanilla. Fold in 1 pint of heavy cream already whipped. Freeze.

Almond Roca
Donna Ericson

1/2 cup water
1 cup white Karo
3 cups sugar
1/2 t. salt

1 # butter
1 # raw white almonds
3 8oz. Hershey bars (24 oz.)

Put sugar and Karo in pan with 1/2 cup water. As soon as it boils, add butter and almonds, stirring constantly, since butter burns easily. Let cook till almonds are brown when dropped into cold water and broken open. Dump directly onto metal cabinet, which has been cleaned completely bare and covered with wide aluminum foil. (This spreads a lot). Cover with Hershey bars and spread evenly when melted. Top with chopped nuts and press down gently.

version 2 - Susan Carter (Water Therapy)

2 cups sugar
1# butter
4 oz. sliced almonds (1 1/4 cups)
1 large (7 oz.) Hershey Milk Chocolate bar
very finely chopped walnuts

Put almonds in oven at 250 degrees.

Combine sugar and butter in pressure cooker size pan and stir
constantly with wooden spoon on medium heat. ingredients will separate but continue to stir. When it all comes together and becomes dark caramel brown, stir in almonds and pour onto an ungreased cookie sheet. Break Hershey into squares and place on hot roca. When it melts, spread with a spatula and sprinkle finely ground walnuts on top and press down gently. When cool, break into small pieces.

Handkerchief Crepes
Donna Ericson

3 eggs
1/2 cup milk
1/2 cup water
3/4 cup flour
1/2 t. salt
1 T. olive oil
1 T. butter
1 cup ricotta cheese
1/2 T. grated orange zest
1/2 cup mini-bittersweet chocolate chips
1 T. sugar
3/4 cup Cointreau

In a medium bowl, combine eggs, milk and water. Add flour and salt; mix well. Stir in oil. Heat a crepe pan over medium heat. Add butter, lightly coating surface. Add 1/4 cup batter. Work pan in a circular motion, spreading batter evenly to edge. When underside is brown, turn with spatula and brown other side. Transfer to plate. Repeat to make 12 crepes. Preheat oven to 450 degrees. In a bowl, mix ricotta, zest and chocolate chips. Place a rounded T. of ricotta mixture over half of each crepe. Fold the other half over filling, then fold in half again to form a triangle. Place crepes in a baking dish. Sprinkle crepes with sugar, bake 8-10 minutes. At the table, pour Cointreau and ignite. Serves 6.

Chocolate Eclairs
Donna Ericson

12 marshmallows – cut small
1 small can hershey's chocolate syrup
1 c nuts

Mix above and let stand 5 minutes. Cream together ¼ c. butter and 1 cup powdered sugar. Beat 3 egg yolks one at a time into butter and sugar. Add 1 tsp vanilla and combine with chocolate mixture. Beat egg whites stiff and fold in. Crush 14 or 16 graham crackers. Put ½ of crumbs in bottom of 9 inch square pan. Pour chocolate mixture on top of crumbs. Put rest of crumbs on top. Let stand in fidge 12 hours. Serve with whipped cream.

Apple Bake
Donna Ericson April 6, 1956

1-1/2 c. sugar
½ c. butter
1 egg
1 c. raw apple chopped
1 c. cold coffee
2 c. flour

½ tsp baking powder
½ tsp salt
½ tsp cinnamon
1 tsp cloves
½ c. nuts or raisins

Cream sugar and butter. Add egg and beat well. Sift dry ingredients and add alternately with coffee. Add nuts and apples last. Mix through batter. Sprinkle some sugar and cinnamon on top and bake at 375 until toothpick in the center comes out clean.

Cream Puffs
Myrna Miller

1 cup water
½ cup butter

1 cup flour
4 eggs

Heat oven to 400. Heat water and butter to boiling in saucepan. Stir in flour, stirring until mixture forms into ball, leaving the sides of the pain. Beat in the eggs, one at a time. Beat mixture until smooth, drop by spoonful onto cookie sheet and bake for 45 to 50 minutes until puffed and dry. Cool and cut in half, remove insides and put anything inside such as custard or whipped cream, putting top back on when done. Drizzle with chocolate on the top.

Chinese Fried Walnuts
Donna Ericson

6 cups water
4 cups walnuts
1/2 cup sugar

salad oil
salt

In 4-quart saucepan over high heat, heat water to boiling; add walnuts and heat to boiling; cook 1 minute. Rinse walnuts under running hot water; drain. Wash saucepan and dry well.
In large bowl with rubber spatula, gently stir warm walnuts with sugar until sugar is dissolved. (if necessary, let mixture stand 5 minutes to dissolve sugar.) Meanwhile, in same saucepan over medium heat, heat about 1" of salad oil to 350 degrees on deep-fat thermometer (or heat oil according to manufacturer's directions in deep-fryer set at 350 degrees.) With slotted spoon, add about half of walnuts to oil. fry 5 minutes or until golden, stirring often. With slotted spoon, place walnuts in coarse sieve over bowl to drain; sprinkle very lightly with salt; toss lightly to keep walnuts from sticking together. Transfer to paper towels to cool. Fry remaining walnuts. Store in tightly covered container. Makes 4 cups.

As in many homes in Butte, preparation of food for Christmas was a huge tradition requiring long hours of cooking, but always resulting in lifelong memories. Certainly amongst those was my grandmother's fudge. To make this fudge, my mom and all of us six kids would help shell nuts, chop them, and then take turns beating the fudge for hours.

Mom's Fudge
(Lilian Beaulieu)
The best!

Butter a 12"x9" pan.
4 cups sugar
3 sq. chocolate, grated
1 t. salt
1 T. flour
4 T. white Karo
2 cups 1/2 & 1/2 or canned milk
2 t. vanilla
4 T. butter

In pressure cooker or heavy saucepan on med. heat, stirring occasionally, boil all ingredients except vanilla, butter and nuts, till

soft ball, 227 degrees on candy thermometer here in Butte (soft ball stage). Remove from heat, add vanilla & butter; do not stir. Cool to lukewarm. Beat until it loses its gloss and starts to set up. Add nuts and pour into buttered pan. Let set and cut into squares.

Taffy
Myrna Miller
An all-time favorite!

To 1 cup of syrup (white or blue Karo syrup) add about 1-1/4 cup sugar, 1 tablespoon vinegar and butter, about the size of a small egg. Boil until it gets nearly brittle in cold water. Then add ¼ tsp baking soda dissolved in cold water (be careful it doesn't run over) and 1 tsp vanilla. (If you use Blue Karo, don't add vanilla). Pour in buttered pan, let cool, but be sure to turn the corners in toward center as they harden first. When cool enough to handle, pull until white. The secret of good taffy is in the pulling. Use as little butter possible on your hands, but use cold water also. Don't use too much of either or your candy will separate. Longer you pull it, the nicer it is.

Tapioca Pudding
Myrna Miller

My favorite!
2 eggs separated
2 c. milk
½ c. sugar
2 tablespoons tapioca
¼ tsp salt
1 tsp vanilla
2 tablespoon sugar

In saucepan, combine egg yolks, reserve whites in separate small mixing bowl and milk, ¼ c. sugar, tapioca and salt to egg yolks. Cook over medium heat stirring constantly until mixture comes to a full boil. Remove from heat. Blend in vanilla. In separate bowl, beat egg white until frothy. Gradually add 2 tablespoons sugar and beat until mixture forms soft peaks. Fold into tapioca mixture just until well blended. Spoon into serving dishes.

Baked Custard
Myrna Miller

Custard is my favorite – for a short time there was a place in Bozeman which actually served homemade real custard ice cream and I have never found better ice cream.

2 eggs
1/3 c. sugar
¼ tsp salt
2 c milk, scalded
Nutmeg

Heat oven to 350 degrees, beat eggs, sugar and salt together slightly. Pour in the hot scaled milk. Strain into 6 custard cups or a casserole dish and set in pan of water. Sprinkle nutmeg over the top and cover tightly before putting into oven. Bake for 30 minutes until knife comes out clean of custard.

Fool Proof Fudge
Donna Ericson

2 cups semi-sweet chocolate chips
1 cup milk chocolate chips
1 can Eagle Brand milk
Dash salt
1/2 to 1 cup chopped nuts
1 1/2 t. vanilla or 2 t. mint flavoring

In large, heavy saucepan melt chips, milk and salt. Stir in walnuts and vanilla. Spread into 8 or 9" sq. pan lined with wax paper. Chill two hours or until firm. Turn onto board. Peel off paper and cut into squares.

Dev's Caramels
Devvi Morgan

These caramels are one of the finest candies you can ever experience eating.

2 cups sugar	1/2 t. salt
1/4 cup butter	3 cups milk
1 cup light Karo	1 t. vanilla

Heat sugar and syrup in 1 cup milk, stirring until dissolved. Cook to firm ball stage. Slowly add second cup of milk and repeat cooking process. Add final cup of milk, salt and butter and cook until a ball tested in cold water is of firmness desired in finished caramel. (each milk stage takes about 10-20 minutes) Remove from heat, add vanilla and pour into buttered 8x8" pan. Cut strips of 1/2", then cut strips into 3/4" pieces of candy and wrap in wax paper cut into squares about 2.5".

Scrabble
Donna Ericson

8 cups Wheat Chex	1/2 t. garlic powder
8 cups Corn Chex	2 cups nuts
8 cups Rice Chex	9 oz. pretzels
1# butter	1 t. celery salt
4 T. Worcestershire Sauce	1 t. onion salt

Mix all ingredients and put in bottom of blue roaster. Bake at 200 degrees for 2 hours stirring gently every 15 minutes. Put in gallon jars and keep in cool, dark place.

Apple Jack
Donna Ericson

2 cups peeled, cored, diced (1/2") tart green apples
1/4 cup raisins
1/4 cup honey
1 t. ground cinnamon
1/4 t. kosher salt
1 T. butter

1 1/3 cups whole milk
1 cup old fashioned oatmeal (not instant)
1 t. vanilla
1/4 cup apple butter
2 10-12" flour tortillas

Combine the apples, raisins, honey, cinnamon and 1/4 t. kosher salt in a medium bowl. Toss well to coat apples evenly. Melt the butter in a large nonstick skillet over med. heat. Add the apples and cook until the apples feel tender when pierced with a fork, 8-10 minutes. Stir in the milk. Gradually stir in the oatmeal. Reduce heat to low and cook until all of the liquid has been absorbed by the oatmeal. 5-7 minutes. Remove from heat and add the vanilla. Divide the apple butter among the tortillas and spread evenly over each tortilla, leaving at least a 1-inch border around the edge. Divide the apple-oatmeal mixture among the tortillas and wrap.

Cannoli Cream
Donna Ericson

Mix 1/3 cup ricotta with 2 T. heavy cream. Set aside.
Whip 1/3 cup heavy cream, 3 T. powdered sugar and pinch of cinnamon. Fold ricotta mixture gently into whipped cream mixture. Refrigerate 30 minutes.

Mascerate raspberries and strawberries and sliced kiwi in juice of 1/2 lemon and 1 T. sugar for 30 minutes.

Put fruit in dessert glasses, top with cannoli cream and top with toasted slivered almonds.

Eggnog
Donna Ericson

6 eggs, separated
3/4 cup sugar
2 cups whipped whipping cream
1 cup milk
2 cups rum, brandy or Southern Comfort
nutmeg

Beat egg whites until stiff and shiny. Beat egg yolks until thick and fluffy; gradually beat in sugar. Add the whipped cream and milk to the yolk mixture, stirring well. Add, still stirring, the liquor. Fold in beaten egg whites. Chill in refrigerator until ready to serve. Dust with nutmeg. Makes 10 servings, about five ounces each.

Growing up as a child, we lived for a short while in Helena, Montana, where there were crab apple trees everywhere; out of one of those trees my older brother fell face first onto the concrete sidewalk below, which I supposed was not as dumb as the few kids who braved the dares to put their tongue on the frozen metal bars of the merry-go-round. Behind our houses also grew wild rhubarb and onions, and next to these lay the cemetery filled with old tombstones, which we had to brave if we wanted the rhubarb or onions. For many years as a young girl, from this cemetery came the monster of my worst nightmares whom I hid from in the kitchen cupboards.

Oatmeal-Rhubarb Crumble
Donna Ericson

Preheat oven to 375 degrees.

4 cups chopped fresh rhubarb (1"pieces), about 4 large stalks
1 1/4 cups sugar, divided
2 T. cornstarch
1/4 t. ground nutmeg
1/3 cup flour
1/2 t. ground cinnamon
1/4 cup margarine
1/2 cup old-fashioned rolled oats

Place the rhubarb in a 1 1/2-quart casserole.

In a small bowl, stir 1 cup of the sugar together with the cornstarch and nutmeg. Pour over the rhubarb and toss.

In a medium bowl, stir together the flour, cinnamon and remaining 1/4 cup sugar. Using a pastry cutter or 2 knives in a scissorlike motion, (I use my hands), cut in the margarine until the mixture resembles coarse cornmeal. Stir in the oats. Sprinkle over the rhubarb mixture. Bake 45 minutes or until the topping is browned and the fruit is cooked.

Rhubarb Swirl
Donna Ericson

3 cups rhubarb
3/4 cup sugar

Mix and let set 1 hour then simmer for 5 to 10 minutes or until tender. Add 1 box (3 oz.) strawberry jello, and stir until dissolved. Cool until syrupy.

Mix together:

1 box (3 oz.) instant vanilla pudding
1 1/2 cups milk
1/4 t. vanilla
8 oz. Cool Whip

Mix and swirl with rhubarb mixture. Pour into graham cracker crust in 9x13" pan. Refrigerate 3 to 4 hours. Serves 6

Divinity
Myrna Miller

Not easy to make and you have to get just right, but every Christmas we made this and it is awesome!

2 c. sugar
½ c + 2 tablespoon syrup
¼ c. hot water
Squirt or two of food coloring as desired

2 egg whites
1 tsp vanilla or almond

Combine sugar, syrup and water and boil to hard ball stage (when you drop a little bit of a spoonful into a cup of cold water, it forms a ball). Slowly add to stiffly beaten egg whites. Beat until dry. Drop on wax paper.

Heavenly Chocolate Fondue
Donna Ericson (from Karen Ericson daughter-in-law)

1 - 14 oz. can sweetened condensed milk
1 - 10 oz. jar marshmallow cream
1/2 cup milk
1 t. vanilla
1 - 12oz. pkg. semi-sweet chocolate chips

Combine all ingredients. Heat until chocolate pieces melt in top of a double boiler.

Best Hot Fudge Sauce
Donna Ericson

Combine 8 oz. chopped semi-sweet chocolate with 7 T. softened butter, 1/2 cup sugar, 1/2 cup heavy cream, and 1/4 cup hot water in the top of a stainless-steel double boiler. Melt chocolate mixture, stirring with a wooden spoon, over simmering water, at medium-low heat, about 5 minutes. Remove from heat, and stir in 1 t. vanilla extract and a pinch of salt. Serve warm over ice cream. Sauce may be stored in the refrigerator for up to one week. Reheat in a microwave oven or double boiler. Makes about 2 cups.

Pineapple-Macadamia Cobbler
Devvi Morgan

Filling:
   3/4 c. sugar
   1/4 c. bisquick
   4 cups bite-size pieces fresh pineapple or other fruit
   1 t. fresh grated lemon peel

Topping:
   1 egg
   2/3 c. sugar
   1/4 c. melted butter or margarine
   3/4 c. bisquick
   1/2 c. sweetened flaked coconut, toasted
   1/2 c. coarsely ch. macadamia nuts

Heat oven to 350. Grease an 8-in. sq. baking dish.
Filling: Mix sugar and baking mix in a large bowl. Add pineapple and lemon peel and toss to mix and coat. Scrape into prepared baking dish. Topping: Whisk egg, sugar and butter until blended and smooth. Stir in bisquick and 1/4 c. of the coconut. Spread over filling to cover completely. Sprinkle with remaining coconut and the macadamia nuts. Bake 40-45 min. until puffed and golden.

Peach Cobbler
Donna Ericson

1 stick butter
1 cup sugar
3/4 cup self-rising flour
3/4 cup milk

one 28oz. can sliced peaches in syrup, undrained (see variations)

Preheat oven to 350 degrees. Put butter in deep baking dish and place in oven to melt. Mix sugar and flour; add milk slowly to prevent lumping. Pour over melted butter. Do not stir. Spoon fruit on top, gently pouring in syrup. Do not stir; batter will rise to top during baking. Bake for 35 - 45 minutes. Good with fresh whipped cream or vanilla ice cream. When available, fresh fruit is wonderful.

Cheese Filled Crepes w/Raspberry Sauce
Donna Ericson

Crepes:
3 eggs	2 T. melted butter
1 1/4 cups flour	Pinch salt
1 1/2 cups milk	1/2 t. lemon extract
2 T. sugar	

Place all ingredients in mixing bowl and beat well with an electric mixer. Let batter stand for 1 hour. Heat non-stick 7-inch saute pan on med. heat until hot. Rub pan with paper towel dipped in melted butter or use a brush. Pour in 2 T. of batter and tilt pan until batter has covered bottom. Heat until the batter begins to cook and edges curl away from sides of pan. Invert onto paper towel and continue with balance of crepes.

Raspberry Sauce:
3 T. sugar
1 pint raspberries

Mash 3 Tablespoons sugar with 1 pint mashed raspberries. Combine berry puree and sugar.

Filling:
3 T. sugar
1 cup cottage cheese
1 t. vanilla
1/2 cup sour cream
1/2 t. grated lemon or orange peel

Mix cottage cheese, sour cream, sugar, vanilla and lemon or orange peel in a bowl. Spoon about 2 T. of cheese mixture onto each crepe. Fold each crepe to seal. Serve cold with Raspberry Sauce.

Donna's Frozen Lemon Dessert
Donna Ericson

4 large eggs	1 pint whipping cream
1 cup sugar	50 vanilla wafers, crumbled. Save 1/3 cup
6 or 7 T. fresh lemon juice	for top

Place wafer crumbs in bottom of 9x13 baking pan. Separate eggs. Beat yolks till foamy. Add sugar gradually and lemon juice. Beat egg whites till firm. Fold yolk mixture into egg whites. Beat cream till stiff, then fold in egg mixture. Blend well, scraping from bottom of bowl. Pour over crumbs. Top with remaining crumbs. Freeze.

Dessert Pizza Pie
Donna Ericson

Crust: 3 cups flour
   3/4 cups powdered sugar
   1 1/2 cups margarine or butter
Blend ingredients together. Divide into half. Spread each half onto a 14" pizza pan. Bake at 325 degrees until light brown - about 15 minutes. Cool.

Filling: for 1 crust. (For 2 crusts, double this recipe)
   1 - 8 oz. Philadelphia Cream cheese
   1/2 cup sugar
   1 t. vanilla
   Blend and spread on cooled crust.

Topping: Use any canned pie filling or fresh fruit. Place on cream cheese filling just before serving.

Slice like pie and serve with a dallop of whipped cream or Cool Whip.

Note: The cookie crust can be made ahead of time and kept at room temp. a couple of days or wrapped and frozen. Add the filling and topping just before serving to keep the crust from becoming soggy. Leftovers do become soggy, but taste good anyway. You don't very often have any leftovers, at least I don't.

APPLE CRISP
Donna Ericson

6 - 8 tart cooking apples
1 T. lemon juice
1/2 cup sugar
1/2 t. nutmeg

1 t. cinnamon
3/4 cup rolled oats
1/2 cup brown sugar
3 T. oil

Core, peel and slice the apples into small pieces. Put the sliced apples in a bowl; sprinkle with lemon juice, sugar, nutmeg and cinnamon; mix. Place the apples in a 9x13 inch baking dish. Combine the rolled oats, brown sugar, flour and oil. Pour evenly over the apples. Bake in a preheated 375 degree oven for 40 minutes or until the apples are tender. 8 servings.

Tradition in my home with my daughters is the making of our own caramel corn every New Year's Eve – no matter where time has taken us since, this caramel corn recipe remains a part of our tradition. This recipe is from my brother's wife in the 70's – it is absolutely the best!

Caramel Corn
Michelle Hunt

10 quarts popped corn. Keep warm in 200 degree oven in big blue roaster.

In large saucepan, melt 1 cup butter. Stir in 1/2 cup light or dark Karo syrup, 2 cups brown sugar and 1 or 2 t. salt. Boil 5 minutes on lowest heat possible without stirring. Remove from heat. Stir in 1/2 t. soda and 1 T. vanilla. Stir fast! Pour over popcorn. (Also use 2 c. peanuts, if desired). Coat well. Put in 250 degree oven for 1 hour, stirring every 15 minutes. Cool. Store air tight.

Creme Brulee
Donna Ericson

In plate, spread 1 cup of light brown sugar to dry out. Set aside. In 1 1/2 quart saucepan, scald 4 cups heavy cream. Split a vanilla bean, scrape seeds and put into cream, also the skins of vanilla bean. Do not boil. In bowl put 6 egg yolks and 1 whole egg. Add 3/4 cup plus 2 T. sugar. Whisk to blend. Then slowly add the hot cream into the mixture and whisk until uniform in color. Strain into a large measuring cup with pouring lip. Preheat oven to 310 degrees. Fill custard cups or molds 1/2 full with mixture. Set molds in jelly roll pan and finish filling to rim. Pour hot tap water into jelly roll pan until it reaches 1/2 way up the molds. Bake 30 minutes. Cool 30 minutes, then refrigerate at least 2 hours. To finish, sprinkle a thin layer of dried brown sugar over the top of each custard and place under broiler till sugar is caramelized. Serve and enjoy!

CHAPTER 8
HINTS
BY DONNA ERICSON

When using the candy thermometer, deduct 8 degrees for here in Butte.......thus 240 degrees would be 232 here in Butte.

To make whipped cream hold its shape....dissolve 1 t. unflavored gelatin in 1 T. hot water. Cool but don't allow to set. Add to whipped cream during last minutes of whipping.

Hint: You will get almost twice the amount of juice if the lemon is dropped into hot water for a few minutes before squeezing or heated in the microwave on med. for 1 min.

Hint: Dough can rise with no problem even in a cold kitchen if the bowl is placed on a heating pad set on medium.

Hint: If the television is in use, it makes a nice warm spot for dough to rise.

Hint: You can clean darkened aluminum pans easily by boiling them in two t. of cream of tartar mixed in a quart of water. Ten minutes will do it.

Hint: Chopped nuts will be more evenly dispersed in batter if they are lightly floured before adding to batter.

Hint: Slip your hand inside a waxed sandwich bag and you have a perfect mitt for greasing your baking pans and casserole dishes.

Hint: If the soup is too salty, add a cut raw potato and then discard it once it has cooked and absorbed the salt.

Hint: Instant soup stock will always be on hand if you save the pan juice from cooking meats. Pour the liquid into ice cube trays and freeze. Place the solid cubes in freezer bags and label.

Hint: Never put a cover on anything that is cooked in milk unless you want to spend hours cleaning up the stove when the pot boils over.

Hint: The easiest way to skim off fat from soup is to chill until the fat hardens on top of the liquid. If time will not permit this, wrap ice cubes in paper toweling and skim over the top.

Hint: To prevent curdling of milk or cream in soup, add the soup to the milk rather than the milk to the soup. Or add a bit of flour to the milk and beat well before combining.

Hint: To prevent soggy salads, place an inverted saucer in the bottom of the salad bowl. The excess dressing will drain under the saucer and keep the greens crisp.

Hint: Lettuce and celery will crisp up faster if you add a few raw slices of potato to the cold water when you soak them.

Hint: Store lettuce and celery in paper bags instead of plastic. Leave the outside leaves and stalks on until ready to use.

Hint: Wrap onions individually in foil to keep them from becoming soft or sprouting.

Hint: Peel garlic and store in a covered jar of olive oil. The garlic will stay fresh and the oil will be nicely flavored for salad dressings.

Hint: To prevent eggs from curdling when they are added to hot liquid, add a bit of the hot liquid to the eggs first and let the temperature equalize. Then they can be added to the remaining liquid with no worries.

Hint: A dripping faucet can be quieted by tying a string to it that reaches into the sink. The water will slide down the string quietly.

Hint: When preparing your favorite casserole, double the batch and freeze one for a busy day.

Hint: If a casserole dish is lined with several layers of aluminum foil and then filled and frozen, the casserole can be lifted out when solid and wrapped for freezing without losing the use of the casserole dish. It will fit right back into the dish when it's time to bake it. This also makes for easier stacking of casseroles in the freezer.

Hint: To reheat a roast or leftover beef or pork, wrap in aluminum foil and heat in a slow oven.

Hint: Baking fish on a bed of celery and onions will add to the taste as well as keep the fish from sticking to the pan.

Hint: An excellent thickener for soups is a little oatmeal. It will add flavor and richness to almost any soup.

Hint: Run a cup of white vinegar through the entire cycle in an empty dishwasher to remove all soap film.

Hint: A quick frosting can be made by adding a bit of chocolate syrup to prepared whipped topping.

When you don't have the right sized pan........

- For a 4-cup baking dish: one 9" pie plate or one 7 3/8x 3 5/8x2 5/8" loaf pan; or one 8"x 1 1/4" round layer-cake pan
- For a 6-cup baking dish: one 10" pie plate; or one 8" or 9"x 1 1/2" round layer-cake pan, or one 8 1/2" x 3 5/8" x 2 5/8" loaf pan
- For an 8-cup baking dish: one 8x8x2" square pan; or one 11x7x1 1/2" baking pan; or one 9x5x3" loaf pan
- For a 10-cup baking dish: one 9x9x2" square pan; or one 11 3/4x7 1/2x1 3/4" baking pan, or one 15 1/2x10 3/4x1" jelly roll pan.
- For 3 8" round pans: two 9x9x2" square cake pans.
- For two 9" round layer-cake pans: two 8x8x2" square cake pans; or one 13x9x2" pan.
- For one 9x5x3" loaf pan: one 9x9x2" square cake pan
- For one 9" angel cake tube pan: one 10x3 1/4" Bundt pan, or one 9x3 1/3" fancy tube pan.

To remove the skins from filberts or hazelnuts: heat in a 350 degree oven for about 10 minutes, pour onto a terry cloth towel and rub gently with the towel. Another way is......in 2 or 3 quart saucepan bring 4 c. water and 1 T. soda to a boil. Add up to 4 cups hazelnuts. Cook 3 minutes. Drain, immerse in cold water and rub between your hands to loosen most of the skin. Drain again and spread on towel to dry. Scrape off any remaining skin with tip of sm. paring knife. Put in single layer in jellyroll pan. Bake at 300 degrees to dry nuts 8-10 minutes. Cool at least 15 minutes, return to oven and toast until golden brown, shaking pan occasionally.

If your hollandaise sauce curdles.....whisk 2 T. of water into 1/4 cup of curdled hollandaise; keep whisking until smooth. Or, if the cooked sauce has just begun to separate, immediately set the pan of sauce in a bowl of ice water to stop the cooking; beat until smooth. Then gently reheat over simmering water.

Cooking with wine:
   White......cauvignon blanc
           chardonay...add a little butter or cream to balance the acidity
   Red........Beaujolais or pinot noir - light red wine sauce
           Cabernet sauvignon or red zinfadel - hearty sauce

The secret to keeping a fruit pie crust from getting soggy is egg white. The proteins bond together and form a wall that prevents the filling's juices from seeping into the crust. Lightly beat an egg white; then brush it over the inside of the uncooked shell before adding the fruit mixture. The coating will set as the pie bakes and keep your dessert crisp.

May you gain many great friends and memories from this book's pictures and recipes as our family has through the many years of living in Butte, America.

From the Three Sisters
Myrna, Alice, and Donna Miller

www.ingramcontent.com/pod-product-compliance
Lightning Source LLC
Chambersburg PA
CBHW081457040426
42446CB00016B/3280